PERENNIALS

*For Thomas MacCubbin,
Horticultural Extension
Agent, Orange County,
Florida, and Joan
MacCubbin.*

The WI Creative Gardening Series
PERENNIALS

John Kelly

UNWIN

HYMAN

LONDON SYDNEY WELLINGTON

First published in Great Britain by the Trade
Division of Unwin Hyman Limited, 1989.

UNWIN HYMAN LIMITED
15–17 Broadwick Street
London W1V 1FP

Allen & Unwin Australia Pty Ltd
8 Napier Street, North Sydney, NSW 2060,
Australia

Allen & Unwin New Zealand Pty Ltd with the Port
Nicholson Press
Compusales Building, 75 Ghuznee Street,
Wellington, New Zealand.

ISBN 0-04-440376-3

British Library Cataloguing in Publication Data
Kelly, John
    Perennials.
    1. Gardens. Perennial flowering plants
    I. Title
    5359'32

Designed by Julian Holland

Typeset by Latimer Trend & Co Ltd
Printed in Great Britain by Butler & Tanner Ltd,
Frome

Acknowledgements
I would like to thank Connie Austen
Smith, Clare Ford, Helen Wythers and
Julian Holland, the designer, for their
assistance.
    The photographs used in this book were
taken by John Kelly (JK), Julian Holland
(JH) and Tony Bates (TB).

Contents

Foreword

Ornamental gardening is undergoing a revolution as significant as the demise of the parterre, the rise of the woodland garden or the advent of the Wardian case. The difference between this and other revolutions is that whereas they could be summed up in a very few words, the present one cannot. Instead, it needs to be defined and, once that has been done, its central theme must be named.

The history of gardening is one of periods in which styles rose and fell in popularity and of a constant increase in the availability of plants. This stream of new introductions has been subject to floods and droughts over the years, but it has never dried up. Today we find ourselves in a new age of plant introductions with air travel making the work of the plant-hunters so much easier.

The plant breeder, too, is spurred on to greater and greater efforts by competition and the availability of techniques unknown to his forebears. Micropropagation, the manipulation of light and the science of genetics have meant that new plants can be produced far more quickly and in larger numbers.

These factors alone, however, do not explain the modern revolution. Social factors are, if anything, of greater importance. In the previous plant-hunting age the recipients of new introductions were, apart from the botanical institutions, the rich, or at least the well-to-do. Even if a nursery, such as that of Veitch, were to receive the greater part of the results of an expedition, the plants would, in the end, be priced far above what an 'ordinary' person of the day could dream of affording.

How all that has changed! Today's ordinary man and woman is widely knowledgeable and, in comparison with the standards of a few decades ago, immensely well off. The cost of plants has come down greatly in real terms and now the gardener can drive the family car to the nearby garden centre and carry away beautifully grown plants in containers to spacious home gardens in which gadgets, growing aids, and means of righting the ills of plants are to be found that would have astounded the gardener of yore.

The gardening media have played a highly significant role. The continuing education of the gardener is effected in several of them. Radio provides a weekly clinic, in which the questions come to be asked more and more by informed people; television programmes reach different levels on the various channels, including what has been called the 'Open University of gardening'; and gardening magazines work to print runs that are truly surprising. That gardening books of high quality are to be found in the great majority of homes is, of course, axiomatic.

The result of all this is a gardening population that has grown enormously in numbers and which brings to bear a great deal of economic weight – it has come to be highly discriminating and aesthetically aware. The flight from the annual chore of sowing, planting, and then clearing up the repetitive bedding plants continues, while, most importantly of all, the intrinsic qualities of plants are being recognised by a wider and wider public. People are now ready to realise that specialisation can be a dead end and that plants do not have to be segregated, one group from another, in some sort of horticultural apartheid.

This, then is the scenario as ornamental gardening stands ready to set off along a path that is not new, but one which has been but sparingly explored. Today's gardeners and those that follow them will increasingly find themselves part of a new movement, in which plants will be regarded, not as mere flower-bearers, but as creations possessed of other aspects of beauty. They are not members of exclusive groups – perennials, alpines, and so on – but are elements in the greater garden population, and should not, therefore, be seen as items to be forced into designs, but as individuals to whom designs must relate.

The central theme of this gardening revolution is creativity. True, it might be maintained with some justification that all gardening is creative, but the word means more than we have been capable of hitherto. Gertrude Jekyll, Vita Sackville-West and Marjorie Fish were all creative, certainly, but their gardening was relatively limited in scope and their designs idiosyncratic. To say as much is not to belittle them; few would deny their greatness, but the path of modern Creative Gardening is being trodden by a few who have seen how to throw off both the constraints of fashion and those imposed by their predecessors; and have recognised the deep philosophical and aesthetic advances that are possible, subtle though they may be.

Modern Creative Gardening is the art of appreciating the qualities of plants – including those that are to be seen when flowers are absent – and putting them into a context of inter-related beauty. It is gardening become art, and it is an art that is accessible to everyone.

This series of books does not address the subject of Creative Gardening directly. It is rather a primer, in which the prevailing conventions are used as starting points from which the reader may progress further. The books follow the divisions, or categories, into which garden plants are (sometimes arbitrarily) put, but they endeavour to lead you, the reader, towards a feeling that such distinctions hold our gardening imaginations back.

That the role of a shrub may be played by a perennial; that the beauty of a drift of bulbs *needs* accompaniment as much as a singer of *Lieder*; and that 'alpines' can be members of any group from bulbs to trees will be apparent to anyone who reads the books in the series. If such a reader then goes on to join the van of today's gardening, then the series will have done its job.

A series of gardening books provides a source of information and, one hopes, interesting reading on those aspects of gardening that you, the particular reader, are interested in. If you purchase a large, encyclopaedic work, you will probably spend a considerable proportion of its price on material that you are unlikely ever to need. It may be that you will not be able to relate to the writer either, especially if there are several.

With the Creative Gardening series you do not have to take them all. If you are content to remain interested in just one or two of the groups of plants, then you can choose just those volumes that deal with them. Whichever course you take, you may be sure that the authors are people who really do garden. They may be specialists in their fields or, like me, generalists with particular favourites and individual ways of looking at things. Whoever you choose to read will be a gardener like you – someone who has been driven to tears by failure, made joyful by success, or rendered bereft of any explanation for the contrariness and sheer mystery of Nature.

My colleagues may be eminent, aesthetically talented, or may, again like me, garden for a living. What we have in common, above all, is a love of plants and of the gardens in which we grow them or just see them growing. Our motivation in writing these books has been a desire to share such things with those who read us.

John Kelly

Series Editor
Abbotsbury, Dorset, 1989

Introduction

Gardening should be a simple, relaxed occupation providing endless pleasure, a great deal of satisfaction and very little worry or fuss. Unfortunately for many people, a great deal of mumbo-jumbo and jargon gets in the way of their enjoyment and they find that success is hidden behind a web of words that seem to mean one thing but often mean another. Too many encounters with experts, *soi-disant* or otherwise, whose vocabularies are larded with words like scion, petiole, callousing and deep-bed system, tend to suggest an academic superstructure that is daunting in the extreme. In fact, it does not exist at all.

What there is instead is a body of garden lore, much of it pseudo-scientific, a lot of it rooted in garden history or in the handing down of thoughts from one generation of gardeners to another, and a good deal of it born of the necessity to find handy labels for plant groupings that man has devised in the face of Nature's divisions. This wisdom has, like that of the old herbalists,

its own vocabulary.

One of the words in it is 'perennial'. To a botanist its meaning is clear enough – it refers to a plant of any kind whose life is extended over a number of years in which it grows, flowers and sets seed. The gardener will agree with this but he will tend to put it another way. He will say that it refers to a long-lived plant or to one that comes up every year. Put the word into the plural, however, and you will find that agreement disappears.

The botanist will stick to his last and submit the same definition of 'perennials' as he did for 'perennial'. The gardener, on the other hand, will become rather confusing and will, if not rendered inarticulate. start to introduce all sorts of qualifications into what *he* means by perennials. He will say, for instance, that perennials are herbaceous plants. Then again he is likely to aver that they are plants that are suitable for borders. Further, he may tell you that perennials are hardy, otherwise they

Although crocosmias grow from corms, their habit leads us to include them among herbaceous perennials (*TB*)

would not be listed as hardy perennials in catalogues and text-books. Finally, when he says that perennials are those plants that are non-woody, you will be tempted to give up and go back to knitting.

The truth is to be found somewhere among all these ideas. Many perennials are herbaceous and die down every year, but many are not and remain leafy all their lives. Such plants can be termed evergreen perennials. Borders are by no means the only places where perennials can be grown, and it has quite escaped our gardener's attention that hardy perennials are so called in order to distinguish them from those that cannot stand frost. Finally, and most contradictory of all, the vast majority of woody plants are perennial. but those plants that we call perennials are not woody.

From these contradictions emerges a definition that we can use with some chance of understanding one another. Perennials, in fact, cannot be neatly categorised by saying what they are; it is the catalogue of what they are not that defines them.

Perennials are those plants that are not trees or shrubs, neither are they bulbs. They cannot be categorised as alpines. They will, for the most part, be hardy in the open garden and thus do not include tender plants that need more than the minimum of winter protection. They are for the most part herbaceous in nature but include among their number some non-woody evergreens.

It is not just amateur gardeners who would benefit from an analysis of the status of the term 'perennials'. Many professionals fail to avoid the pitfalls that await them. For instance, *Phormium tenax*, the New Zealand flax, is almost always included in lists of shrubs, although it is an evergreen perennial, while what is perhaps the most prestigious dictionary of gardening in the English language persists in calling *Crocosmia masonorum* a herbaceous plant, while notable works on bulbs include it because it grows from a corm.

Perhaps, after all, such authorities are just like the rest of us who when pressed, say, 'Well . . . you *know* what I mean.'

The History of Perennials in Gardens

Learned books on garden history tend to concentrate on the large gardens that were owned by the rich and powerful. This approach is academically the best, not least, perhaps, because ordinary working people could only garden in the simplest ways.

A couple whose every waking hour was spent hard at work, either in earning a living or in making clothes and feeding their family, could not afford to be concerned with such ideas as garden design. Still less could they think about what categories the plants in their garden might fall into. The food plants were the most essential, especially to families who lived in the country and whose plot of land was often part of their wage. Top fruit (apples, pears and so on) were grown, so trees had their place in the garden, but soft fruit was, until comparatively recently in history, obtained from the hedgerows and from uncultivated banks.

Flowers were grown too. Their presence in the garden was almost entirely a result of practical considerations – it is a bonus when a runner bean's flowers look pretty, not a necessity – and the flowers of such things as lavender, rosemary and chives would have been familiar to almost everyone before the industrial revolution. Plants were grown to flavour food as well as to provide it, and we tend to forget that our carefully hygienic world saves us from having to make decisions about keeping foodstuffs that may not be quite as fresh as our palates would like. Furthermore, the countryside was not the fragrant place that it generally is today. The odd whiff of farmyard slurry and the occasionally pervasive smell of motor car exhausts are nothing to the reeks that assailed the noses of our forebears. Sanitation was unknown in the cottages of the hard-working country people and the night soil was too valuable as a fertiliser for it merely to be disposed of.

It is similarly unthinking of us to imagine that people were anything other than smelly themselves. Soap was a luxury and the cottager and his wife would use the soapwort, *Saponaria officinalis*, in its place. Its flowers are very pleasant and its close relatives can be seen in the rock gardens of today. Merely to try to be clean was a major task. Fleas, lice, cockroaches and all kinds of other horrors infested human dwellings, so that plants that were inimical to them took honoured places in the garden. Fleabane, which was strewn in the bed to deter fleas, might very well have been found growing next to plants whose pleasant perfumes must have been greatly treasured.

That there was no design element is not true. Man has an innate love of beauty and of order and the two together make for an impulse towards attractive arrangements. Cottage gardens were indeed beautiful and their tradition was handed down through many generations, particularly of women, for whom the opportunity to make existence more bearable must have been a godsend.

In creating colourful gardens in which design played a part, albeit a subsidiary one, there would have been no reason to separate plants into the woody and non-woody or into the herbaceous and the evergreen. Plants were plants and they were placed where they were most convenient for the family or where they would grow best. Next in priority came aesthetic considerations which, although of the least, were not of little importance. The result was a kind of ordered jumble, in which cabbages might jostle sops-in-wine and carrots thrive in company with marigolds. Often such associations were good for the plants and became traditional. More frequently serendipity played a full part.

Those plants that we have defined as perennials grew happily, if a trifle haphazardly, among trees, shrubs and bulbs in tightly-packed, small plots where the hum of bees, often from the family's own hive, accompanied the pollination that led to the setting of the all-important seed. There was not a lot of time for vegetative propagation and the forms and strains were to a large extent those that could be grown easily from seed, although their perpetuation by division was highly desirable.

Meanwhile, up at the big house, leisure was allowing a different attitude towards and *raison d'être* for gardening. Various social influences demanded that ornamental gardens be attached to houses – sometimes for such reasons as the desirability of somewhere attractive to walk of an evening while great matters were discussed. Often, though, they were simply manifestations of keeping up with the Joneses.

Where informality ruled in the cottage garden, the higher classes tended towards and ever-increasing formality of layout and content. Over the centuries styles changed so that we now label them as Renaissance, Italianate, and so on, but the urge to formalise was never swept away. Even Lancelot Brown's capabilities were not that effective. Gardens in which there was space for leisure activities had that space delineated by borders and punctuated by beds.

Beds eventually became the domain of annual plants, while perennials dominated the borders. Low-growing annuals did not interrupt the view across the leisure space, while tall perennials could be allowed to stand against the walls and hedges that bounded it. If they were graduated in height so that the shortest were in front, so much the better. The herbaceous border was born from the availability of leisure to the moneyed classes, as were the terms bed, border, bedding plant and perennial. The formalisation of the herbaceous border reached, as did that of the bed, into the gardens of the industrial middle class that came into property-owning during the nineteenth and twentieth centuries. The cottage garden was not something that these folk wished to emulate, as they had leisure. Their leisure time was on a small scale, but so were their properties, so gardens developed with the lawn as leisure-space, surrounded or bounded by borders in which 'border plants' grew. Simultaneously, beds and borders became interchangeable concepts and it was possible to see perennials growing in beds, while borders sported annuals. Nevertheless, 'bedding plants' are annuals to this day.

It is only very recently indeed that the role of perennials as plants that have legitimate places in all sorts of habitats in the garden has become generally recognised. We are much more enlightened and practical about formalisation and about rigid adherence to categories, and we tend now to look at plants as plants and to put the woody with the non-woody and the herbaceous with the evergreen.

The vastly increased plant knowledge possessed by today's home gardeners, the greatly increased range of available plants, and the habit of thinking less rigidly about almost everything have wreaked a revolution in gardening, one result of which is that perennials find themselves partners in another sort of association. It has something of the joyful jumble of the cottage garden, but it is one in which the plants can truly come into their own as members of the harmonious plant community, instead of being cordoned off into self-limiting, artificial groupings.

This is the mixed border, a place which may really be a bed, but no matter. In it shrubs, trees, bulbs and perennials grow together in neighbourly harmony. The extension of this concept is the viewing of the garden as an entity, a larger canvas than the border, upon which can be carried out grander designs in which the plants are truly set free at last and given something like the environment that Nature intended.

The Modern Perennial

Perennials comprise such a large and diverse 'class' of plants that it would seem at first glance rather unproductive to try to discuss characteristics that they might have in common. What on earth, one might ask, has *Eryngium planum*, a somewhat thistle-like plant, got that makes it even remotely akin to the mighty jungle-dweller, *Gunnera manicata*? Or how can one possibly speak in the same breath of *Hemerocallis* 'Golden Chimes' and *Primula* 'Inverewe'?

The answers to these questions are rather nebulous. A plantsman or plantswoman (I intend henceforth to use the masculine form inclusively, as in 'mankind', otherwise the whole thing will become a bore) will tend to wallow a bit, using words like 'presence' and 'habit' without really saying much that will help. In fact, it is just these things that distinguish good plants from those that are merely mediocre and those whose sole ornamental function is to act as flower-bearers.

Plantsmen are unimpressed by flowers taken in isolation. They may look wonderful in floral arrangements and are certainly objects of beauty for the most part, but plants need to have more to offer than bloom if they are to be allowed room in what is, for most of us, a finite if not a confined space. It is characteristics other than the colour, shape and size of its flowers that distinguish the garden-worthy perennial. In addition to the three already mentioned there are its foliage, the relationship between size of flower and size of plant, the length of its flowering season and, finally, something indefinable that can only be termed 'character'.

The more abstract elements can, it is true, be subjected to deep and prolonged analysis by those who have the time and inclination for such academic pursuits. There is little point in going to all that trouble, though, as anyone who has any pretensions towards gardening or the slightest comprehension of taste is going to know character, style or presence when she or he sees them. The tangible assets of plants are, however, well worth examining.

Foliage is of the greatest importance in perennials, even more so than in trees and shrubs, in whom brightly-coloured branchlets and interesting bark can play such strong roles. As well as shape and size, colour comes to the fore and it is all too seldom appreciated by gardeners that to arrange plants according to the colours and shapes of their leaves is almost as vital as to do so according to the colours of their flowers. One may indeed see many borders in which everything that can possibly be said to have golden foliage has been crammed, and there are, I fear, far too many so-called white gardens in which dirty greys rule the roost. How often, though, does one see perennials planted in ways which suggest that the many shades of green have been taken into account?

The size and shape of foliage are much more often used to good effect. Indeed, it is impossible to garden with perennials in anything other than the most free cottage style if they are not. Only the most untidy mind can tolerate a disordered jumble of

Above: Hardy geraniums in an informal, mixed border – a typically modern planting (*TB*)

Right: Gentiana asclepiadea, the willow gentian, has elegance and style enough for it to be esteemed a plant, and not just for its flowers (*JH*)

Above: Rheum palmatum, whose foliage would be an asset to the garden even if it never flowered (*TB*)

Right: The new Galaxy achilleas display modern, strong colours (*TB*)

leaves; the contrasts and juxtapositions may vary from the simplistic to the complex, but order will almost always be imposed in the interests of beauty.

The matter of balance between the size of a plant and that of its flowers is more delicate than it would at first appear. Too large a flower on too tall a stem will be at the mercy of wind, rain, and any other destructive forces, and the structural strength of the stem will be an important factor. Small flowers on long stems look weedy, while large blooms on short stems can be ravishing. They can also, as in *Gaillardia* 'Goblin', appear quite inappropriate when large, flamboyant flowers huddle down in the manner of modest alpines. It is in this relationship as much as in anything that 'style' becomes recognisable, but that is not all that style is.

The length of flowering season is a major factor in our acceptance of a perennial into the gardens of today. Something like a hosta or *Veratrum nigrum*, whose leaves are so thoroughly delightful, may well be considered to be plants whose flowers are of such little importance that they would not be missed if they failed to occur at all. However, most perennials are grown primarily for their flowers and we tend to dismiss those whose flowering season is short in favour of plants that will provide us with colour over a season rather than for a week or two.

The modern perennial is subject to demands that are of quite different natures than those that applied in days gone by. Even the laced pinks of the weavers of Paisley and the auriculas of the Pennine slopes have succumbed largely to cultural changes among us. We no longer grow perennials primarily for use, neither are they the subject, for most of us, of competition and novelty. We are the heirs, whether we like it or not, of the drive towards leisure and are privileged to stand at a point in history when all but the unhappy few can indulge in aesthetics in their gardens.

Today's plant must satisfy us both in and out of flower, but it must not be vulgar. We have learned that overindulgence by breeders can produce the horticultural equivalent of the more grotesque kinds of dogs, in which huge blossoms of geometrical perfection, if no other, unfurl atop stems and leaves which have not been asked to develop in any kind of proportion. We have grown out of this but our standards of flower size and form are high and rising. We will no longer put up with wishy-washy colours – the mauves of the mid-century make us mock – and we ask that our perennials shall not fall prey to diseases, otherwise we shall dig them up and never grow them again.

Given all that we ask of perennials, it is just as well that there is now a truly vast range of plants that are available to us and from which we may make our demanding choice. That great numbers of gardeners are unaware of this is a cause for sadness and for the depressing sameness that afflicts so many of our gardens even in this educated and enlightened age.

Finding Plants

It has been said fairly often that the availability of plants is subject to supply and demand and it may well seem superfluous to repeat the cliché. Nevertheless it is true that the bland, repetitious selection of plants that is available at most trade outlets is the outcome of economic pressures.

It is, after all, in the seller's interest to stock lines that he is reasonably sure of selling out of. Only the nurseryman of old could carry items that were speculative and, even so, he was sensible enough to know that such things were subsidised by the high prices that he was able to charge. For it is a fact that plants are now relatively much cheaper than they were 30 years and more ago. Nevertheless, there has been a reaction to the supermarket approach to the growing of hardy nursery stock and we are now seeing a renaissance of the specialist nurseryman.

Not that the media have encouraged this. The gardening gurus on the television, or those whose medium is print, tend to enjoin us to pop round to our friendly neighbourhood garden centre for everything that they recommend. If they were to further the cause of mail order and that of the dedicated plantsman-nurseryman on occasion they would be doing everyone a favour. Nobody would ask that they ignore the larger outlets – merely that they should recognise that such places are not the only sources of plants.

When it comes to perennials, the great wealth that awaits us is not to be found among the bales of peat and this week's bargain. Taking all the garden centres in the country together might allow us to make a reasonable choice, but it would be little better than that which could be made from just one or two pure nurserymen and it would be less wide than that which would become available were we to investigate still other sources.

There is no doubt that the richest veins are to be found in the various garden and plant societies, whether they be local or national. Local garden clubs and horticultural societies are great fun, holding interesting meetings and hosting many a fine speaker. The really important role that they play is in the promotion of the circulation of unusual plants. It is at such evenings that one may find oneself able to swap or to buy a rare laced pink or a much sought-after viola and witness the existence of plants that have not been seen in the trade for many a year.

National societies fall into a general group and a particular one. The general societies are based on regions or on causes – the Northern Horticultural Society, for instance, is national, even though it is regionally centred, while the Royal Horticultural Society is, of course, truly national. Those which serve causes are such organisations as the National Council for the Conservation of Plants and Gardens (NCCPG for short, thank heaven!) and among them there may well be rich pickings indeed.

Membership of societies should never be embarked upon in anything other than a spirit of co-operation, however. It is no good thinking that you can take all the time without giving, and the source of the gifts that you can make to others is seed in the first instance. Later on you will be able to hand out cuttings and divisions of your plants with that truly humble mien that all superior gardeners cultivate as a cover for their pride, but for the time being seed will afford a quick method of stocking up with plentiful amounts of swap-bait.

The general societies have seed lists and their members are usually entitled to a number of packets free, after which they must buy. Many of these, such as that of the Hardy Plant Society, are first class, but the choicest morsels are to be found among the specialist societies.

It is worth having been warned that to

develop a specialist interest in gardening is to court eccentricity on a grand scale. Such interests may extend from a strange and almost pathological enthusiasm for green flowers to a permanent excursion into monoculture as one genus takes over. The gardening graveyard is littered with memories of those who have passed on to the obsessive culture of every last hemerocallis, or whose gardens themselves resemble the burial grounds of myriads of tiny animals, in which the bare soil of winter, littered with forlorn labels, evokes comparison with little headstones.

Nevertheless, the judicious use of membership of specialist societies comprises an Open Sesame to the world of rarer plants and is something that should not be eschewed, no matter how hideous the dangers may be. There are a few enlightened and commercially clever people who have discovered how to compile accurate seed lists of immense variety while succeeding in making a living from it. To browse through their lists – usually without pictures because they are not necessary – is to experience anticipation at its keenest. There is no substitute for the delight of growing plants from seed, but a great many of our modern perennials will not come true and have to be propagated vegetatively. That it is a simple procedure with most plants is a boon and it helps to make gardening with perennials such a pleasurable and homespun pastime.

Nobody should be afraid of ordering plants by post. Those nurseries that offer the facility are usually specialist ones whose products will not be available to you otherwise, unless you are prepared to make long journeys. While there have been cases of short-lived businesses that gave poor services, the seeker after interesting perennials will find that there are quite a few firms whose reputations are not only superb but are also of very long standing. To send for their catalogue may be the first step in a relationship that will last for many years and bring unending pleasure. As one who once sold plants by post I can tell you that such nurserymen value their customers highly, even though they may never have met many of them.

It is not too fanciful to suggest that, in addition to widening your gardening experience, a deeper interest in perennial plants is likely to enrich your life at the social and intellectual levels as well.

Growing Conditions

Gardeners will usually find themselves confronted with a fundamental choice, although they may not always recognise it. The decision lies between allowing the plants to dictate the way the garden is to be designed and letting the conditions in various parts of the garden be the dominant factors in the placing of the plants.

The way the decision is made is often an indication of whether the gardener is primarily a designer or a plantsman. The designer will instinctively try to make the plants fit in with his plans, while the plantsman will be concerned that the plants should enjoy the right conditions, at the same time giving very little thought indeed to design considerations. A harmonious garden will be made by someone who combines elements of both, and growing conditions will play a leading part in determining what his garden will eventually look like.

Chief among the factors that make or break a garden is the soil. That it should be understood as much as possible is most desirable; unfortunately the great majority of gardeners have been brought up on a diet of myth and misinformation and lifetimes have been spent in gardens whose soils have been of totally different natures to those assumed by their owners.

The three essential things to get sorted out about soils are their lightness or heaviness, their drainage, and their degree of acidity or alkalinity. Once these are understood, all else follows.

Light soils are those in which the soil particles are relatively large. Sandy soils are very light, while loamy ones are considerably less so. Clay soils are the heaviest. Many alluvial soils, composed mainly of silt, behave like heavy soils because, although they may be light in terms of actual weight per spadeful, their particle sizes are small. Chalk soils – a phenomenon unknown over the greater part of the earth's surface but common in southern England and northern France – are in a category of their own and need to be discussed separately.

Drainage is of the utmost importance. Any soil, no matter what its particle size,

Above: The author's
favourite penstemon, *B.
ovatus*, circulates mainly
among gardeners,
although he obtained it
from a small nursery (*TB*)

Right: Penstemon ovatus
is short-lived, but it is
easily raised from seed
(*TB*)

will fail to support a healthy population of
ornamental plants if it is badly drained.
What happens to plants in waterlogged
soils is that they drown. Drowning is a
process whereby water takes up the spaces
which should be occupied by air, and these
spaces amount to just about half of the
total volume of a given sample of a good
garden soil.

In a well-drained soil, as in any other,
carbon dioxide gathers in these soil spaces,
having been partly produced by the roots
of the plants and partly by the soil bac-
teria. Rain, as it passes downwards
through the soil, flushes this gas out and
draws downwards behind it a supply of
fresh, oxygenated air. If this process is
impeded by waterlogging, then the plants
will die.

A similar fate awaits plants that are
forced to grow in a soil from which air is
excluded in other ways. To allow 'capping'

– in which an impermeable crust is formed on the surface by artificial watering or by a winter's rain on bare soil – is to prevent the downward passage of incident rain and to cause drought conditions as well as those of asphyxiation. To cause compaction of the soil is, of course, to eliminate the spaces which would have held the air and the water by turns.

Heavy soils will soon be reduced to capped, compacted porridge by their being worked in wet conditions, while light ones can be 'got on' much more often. However, many gardeners who have light,

sandy soils also find that they have severe drainage problems. These are usually caused by a phenomenon called podsolisation which involves the formation of a hard, panned layer, rich in the chemicals that have been leached from the soil above, which is totally impermeable. There is no alternative to digging down to this layer and breaking it up.

A heavy soil whose drainage is poor will always be a millstone round the neck of the gardener. There is no point whatever in attempting to garden on such a soil unless you have a passion for couch grass, this-

Phlox paniculata 'Windsor' cannot be grown from seed, but is kept 'true' when propagated from root cuttings. These are taken in late winter (*JH*)

tles, fat hen, and other pernicious weeds. To make a garden of it will necessitate earthworks involving the laying of proper land drains. It is no good listening to those who tell you that the job can be done by adding peat, sand, or anything else. Such measures are excellent in the long term for lightening the soil, but as we have now seen, light soils are not necessarily well-drained.

There is a good deal of confusion about the types of soils that are acid and those that are alkaline. Many gardeners are under the impression that clays are all acid, while others think that they are all alkaline. Neither assumption is true; there are clays that are both, just as sands, silts and loams can be either. On balance, the hardest soils to work are acid clays, while the easiest are alkaline sands, but what the chemical status of your soil is cannot be guessed. It should be measured properly.

The scale on which this measurement is expressed is the familiar pH scale. Unfortunately, it is seldom explained properly, with the result that many gardeners reach wrong conclusions from its use. It is a scale which expresses the reciprocal of the concentration of hydrogen ions in the soil (an index of acidity and alkalinity) in which pH 7 is neutral and numbers lower than that are acid, higher are alkaline. Two fallacies are common. One is that the scale is linear. It is not; it is logarithmic. This means that a soil with a pH of 5 is not one sixth (or even one seventh, as some suppose) more acid than one with a pH of 6; it is 10 times more so. The other fallacy is more understandable, in that it supposes that horticultural neutrality is the same as the chemical value. In fact, although pH 7 truly is neutral, lime-hating plants will not thrive unless the value is well below that in logarithmic terms. A pH below 6 is desirable if a full range of lime-haters is to be grown.

The fact that the scale is logarithmic should be taken into account if you are thinking of testing your soil using one of the tests that can be bought. Accuracy, when one unit on the scale means a 10-fold difference in the result, is paramount and you are much better off having your soil professionally tested. You can, of course, save yourself a lot of money and grief by having a snoop round the neighbourhood. If there isn't an azalea in sight it is unlikely that your attempts to grow *Meconopsis*

will come to anything; pH can go hang. So it is no good adding a bit of peat to a limy soil and expecting it to grow rhododendrons – you need bales and bales of the stuff. Luckily for those concerned with perennials, they are mostly indifferent as to pH, but many of the companion plants that we will be suggesting are not.

Chalk is a soft kind of limestone that was formed at the bottoms of ancient oceans by the deposition of the shells of minute sea-creatures. The soil above it is usually very shallow – sometimes only a very few inches in depth – and it does not behave like other soils. It can work very light when dry, but be greasy when wet. Luckily it dries out extremely quickly, but this is its gravest disadvantage

Because of the shallowness of the soil over chalk, and because its essentially light structure allows it to dry so quickly, it can become very hot in summer and a great many plants which can otherwise tolerate lime in the soil find such conditions intolerable. It is, therefore, a distinction with an important difference that is made between plants that do not like lime (alkaline soils, in other words) and those that do not like chalk soils *per se*.

Few, if any, soils will grow ornamental plants satisfactorily without the addition of fairly copious amounts of plant food or, more accurately, food precursors. Bulky vegetable matter is far better than artificial fertilisers alone, as it greatly assists in maintaining the soil profile – the texture and essential character of the soil. If such materials are enriched by the presence of animal manures, so much the better. I am afraid that there is no substitute for good garden compost or for stable or farmyard manure. In theory inorganic chemicals may be adequate; they are far from it in practice.

Plant-food precursors are such things as straw, leaves and peat that have not yet broken down. Plant foods themselves are inorganic, but they are derived from organic materials. There is no food value in peat. It is the products of its breakdown that are nutritious to plants.

The amount of light that reaches a plant and also the amount of heat are vital to its health. When we speak of a plant requiring a position in full sun we are really recognising its need for a large quantity of light and warmth. Light can be supplied artificially in short, intense bursts in certain horticultural practices (such as the year-round growing of chrysanthemums) because it is the amount and not the duration of light that is important. Light and heat together have a great deal to do with the induction of flower buds, the hardiness of plants, the colour of flowers, the maintaining of their being 'in character', and their general health.

It is not just on the positive side that this is so. Many plants do require a good deal of light and warmth for their well-being, but equally there are many that need relief from them. This has much to do with the adaptation of their counterparts in the wild to the situations in which they have found themselves for thousands of years, and it is inextricably tied up with a fundamental law of plant life. This law states that water lost by the leaf must never exceed water gained by the root. In other words, a plant used to living in shady jungles, where it was able to develop large, soft leaves, will soon be out of sorts if it is placed in a sunny border because the demand made by its leaves for the replacement of water lost by evaporation can never be met by the roots, whose lives have always been easy in the moist soils of the wild forest.

Heat and temperature should not be confused. The air temperature in a sunny situation and that in the shade nearby may be identical; what will be greatly different will be the amount of heat received by each area. Temperatures measured in the sun are meaningless for this reason, as they merely indicate the reaction of the instrument to insolation and not to temperature at all. An understanding of this will help you to appreciate better the behaviour of plants in their environments and the reasons for such things as the success attained in Scottish gardens with such cool-loving plants as *Nomocharis, Primula* and *Meconopsis* than in England, where the amount of heat incident upon them is greater, even though the temperatures may not be all that different.

Moisture is, according to the fundamental law cited above, closely bound up with heat and light. This is not by any means the only reason why some plants need more moisture than others, but it is an important one. Generally speaking, the larger the leaf the more likely it is that a plant will require some shade for its successful cultivation, and the smaller it is the greater is the likelihood of toleration of sun and dry conditions.

Perennials, if they are to be grown happily, will be placed in the best or most ideal soil for their requirements. They will be planted according to their liking of sun or shade, and their need for moisture will be taken into consideration. Within these parameters, the designs of their homes may be made and beds, borders and other places made ready for them.

Armed with a wide choice of plants and with ample sources from which to obtain them, a better appreciation of the elementary principles that govern their needs, and a willingness to let these factors be major ones in the drawing up of the garden design, the gardener can set foot confidently on the long road of contentment that is the reward for the understanding and harmonious cultivation of this most interesting group of garden plants.

Left: Moisture-loving plants like *Primula florindae* must have good drainage. If the water in the soil is stagnant, they will drown (*TB*)

Right: The Himalayan blue poppies will not tolerate limy soils. This is *Mecanopsis* x *sheldonii* (*TB*)

Right: Candelabra primulas need some shade, otherwise they will wilt as water lost from their large, soft leaves exceeds the amount the roots can obtain (*TB*)

Part One

Perennials in Sun

Chapter 1
Borders

Historically, borders were always sunny places. The sunny aspect of the 'big' house was where the flower garden was to be found, and there would normally have been borders against the walls of the house or against hedges placed at right-angles to the main wall. Shady borders were not thought of really, because such an arrangement only called for one if the house was furnished with a walled quadrangle on its sunny side – a most unusual arrangement. Such enclosures were to be found extending from the shady sides, it is true, but they were used primarily as vegetable gardens, while cut flowers for the house would usually be grown in lines.

Nowadays we use the terms 'border' and 'bed' as if the two were interchangeable. It would be much clearer if we did not, and the discriminate use of the terms would encourage us to remember that the two kinds of structure require quite different treatments. The border, because it always has a wall or a hedge behind it, can only be seen from a limited range of aspects and, to have any effect, it needs to have its plants ranged in height from the tallest at the back to the smallest at the front. The bed, however, can be viewed from every angle and demands a much more sophisticated approach to its planting.

Traditionally, the bed was the preserve of annual plants and perennials reigned in the borders, mainly because their considerable heights were best catered for where they would not interrupt internal views. Today, we are much less hidebound and both beds and borders are found under mixed plantings as well as in their more traditional roles.

For those who admire the tradition of the border and for whom an unsurpassed blaze of colour during the summer is ample reward for having bare soil in winter and a form of gardening that is quite demanding as far as labour goes, the herbaceous border has no peer.

Right: Sedum spectabile, a plant designed by nature for growing in sun, but one which looks slightly out of place in a formal border (*JH*)

The Herbaceous Border

It is fashionable among professional gardeners to pronounce the end of the herbaceous border because it is far too labour intensive and something that can only be considered in large gardens. This is all very well, but they overlook the fact that a lot of people actually enjoy working in their gardens and rather like the exercise. Furthermore, the cult of the small garden among gardening communicators, admirable though it may be in its recognition of the fact that the majority of gardens are small, completely excludes the many people who have gardens large enough to sport herbaceous borders quite happily.

The other main criticism of the herbaceous border is that its glory is short-lived. This is true up to a point, in that it will be a bare piece of soil from mid-autumn until the following late spring, but glory is the right word, as no other garden feature can supply such sheer intensity of colour during the summer months. Neither is it true to say that the plants are short-lived in their flowering. From the vast range that is available to us we can choose plants with flowering seasons that are longer than those of a great many much-vaunted shrubs. How much better off is the owner of a well-planned herbaceous border than the rhododendron fan whose main flowering season is considerably shorter?

Today, because we understand the cultivation of bulbs so much better, the herbaceous border can be a colourful place in the spring. If bulbs are planted at a depth greater than that at which they are liable to be disturbed by being forked among, they can lie permanently below the herbaceous plants. If they are displaced by the operations involving dividing and moving, then they themselves can be divided and moved, because, as we now appreciate, it is by no means fatal to bulbs for them to be moved even after they have started to put forth roots. It is just a matter of being careful and, of course, of not allowing any such young roots to become even momentarily subject to dryness.

There can be no denying the sheer productivity of plants like the varieties of *Osteospermum*, the beautiful, iridescent South African daisies whose constancy in milder areas is an annual marvel, nor the seemingly endless (although it is only to be measured in months) blooming of *Oenothera missouriensis* There is no excuse for accepting the idea that the herbaceous border relies entirely on successions of flowering. They are used, it is true, but in the context of the often astonishingly long production of individual plants.

Preparation

Those who would take on the making of a herbaceous border would do well to examine their capacity for hard work at the very beginning. It can be assumed that they will not begin the project without being the sort of people to whom work in the garden is welcome, but they may be surprised to know what is involved at the start. There is no short cut to adequate preparation of the site, but what you should appreciate is that a lot of work at the beginning is going to mean far less in the future.

The border is, I fear, going to have to be dug. The way this should be begun is by taking out a trench one spit deep at one end and carting the soil round to the other. The bottom of the trench should then be broken up and loosened with a fork to the depth of another spit before as much manure or garden compost as you can possibly afford is put into the trench. The spits from the next trench are then put forward on top of the manure, and so you progress down the border. When you reach the end the purpose of the barrowing of the contents of the first trench becomes clear; it is so that they can be used to fill up the final one.

You might be tempted to think that it will be enough to enrich the immediate planting hole for each plant with manure, but you would be making a great mistake in giving in to such an easygoing idea. All you will succeed in doing is in making yourself green with envy when you see the borders of those who have done the job properly and in storing up for yourself inevitably the job of removing everything and starting again. Of course, plants will certainly grow if their border has not been double-dug; they will just not grow as lushly and healthily as they would have done if it had. Furthermore, they will need watering rather often – a requirement that is alien to the well-prepared border. It would, naturally, be folly if you were naïvely to think that double-digging and manuring in preparation then absolved you for ever from adding manure to the border. What it does allow you to do is to apply further enrichment by means of mulching.

It was maintained by the old school of professional gardeners – wonderful men, but given to living by a body of rules and regulations as bizarrely rigid as the law codes of the more obscure banana republics – that the plants should be removed from the herbaceous border every three years and the ground be double-dug and manured yet again. Near-perfect cultural conditions no doubt resulted, but it is not difficult to imagine just how many herbaceous borders there would be in existence today if such a business were indeed essential. An annual mulch with the same manure material that is usually available to you will do perfectly well. It will in time be drawn down to the level of the roots of the plants by the actions of earthworms and by the rain washing downwards the chemical results of its decomposition. Meanwhile it will assist in lowering the soil's water requirements and will keep weeds down.

The other most vital matter during the embryo days of the border is the preparation of yourself. For many reasons you are likely to want to plant the border in the autumn, a time when suitable days for getting on the land are becoming fewer. To have your plants selected and their places planned is essential.

A few years ago, I constructed a large herbaceous border and then went through the catalogue of a firm who supply open-ground herbaceous plants by post. I worked out how many plants I needed and sent my order off but then forgot all about the whole thing until, some months later, about 1,000 plants arrived one morning, all neatly packed in straw in boxes. It was November and the soil was in perfect condition for planting, although the weather forecast was for rain that was likely to persist for a long enough period to preclude planting for several days, if not for weeks. It was a matter of unpacking and planting as soon as possible.

Unfortunately, the planting plan had been in my head and I had never got to putting it on paper. As a result my gallant helpers spent a long day planting like demons while I tried my best to lay the material out in what might turn out to have been an aesthetically pleasing order. Over 1,000 plants, mostly in fives or sixes of each sort, went in, and luckily I got it reasonably right. The odd juxtaposition of orange poppies with magenta peonies has had to be ironed out since, and the years have seen the saving of plants that were being hounded from existence by over-exuberant neighbours, but I shall never do such a thing again and would do everything to encourage you to make your plans on paper. You will make mistakes, but you are not as likely to make ones that will make you cringe every time you see the results.

Choosing and Planning

Your choice of plants will be from among those you already have – either raised from seed, given to you by friends, or bought – and those to be found in catalogues or from among the limited range at the local garden centre. However it is made up, it is a very good idea indeed at this stage to integrate the plants from all sources into a comprehensive plan.

The two most important considerations will be the sizes of the plants and the colours of their flowers. It is pretty obvious that you cannot plan to include a plant if you have no idea of how tall it is going to be or of how far and how quickly it is likely to spread. In many other forms of gardening, flower colour is not of such paramount importance. Indeed, there are arguments for placing flowers second to foliage in some cases, but herbaceous borders are above all enclaves of sheer colourfulness. Foliage will certainly play its part in the herbaceous border, but it will be a secondary one.

Planning by colour in the first instance is a poor idea. A gardener who has a good sense of colour may well be tempted to draw the border to scale and then, in the manner of certain kinds of gardening encyclopaedias, to divide it up into neatly equal areas, each of a colour, and each then labelled with the name of the plant that will provide that colour. Unfortunate results of this method are often seen, as when 12 in high (0.3 m) groups of *Tradescantia virginia* lurk unnoticed behind 2 ft (0.6 m) thickets of *Monarda* 'Prairie Night'. I believe that the best way to plan is to assemble your books and catalogues and then to list the plants that are obtain-

Orange-red is a colour that needs care in its placing. *Papaver orientale* 'Picotee' could cause a disaster if planted thoughtlessly (*TB*)

able by you and which you like. The next step is to assemble lists of these plants according to their heights. You can divide them into tall, medium and short, or into those with ultimate heights that fall within certain measurement limits in feet or centimetres, whichever you are accustomed to using. The border plan will be divided into bands representing these groups of heights and, starting with the band representing the tallest at the back, you start to allot spaces to them according to their spread and colour.

Most good catalogues will give you an accurate idea of the amount of spread you can expect from each plant in good conditions. Some will actually recommend how many of each will properly occupy one square yard or metre. It is as well to follow these suggestions, as only occasionally will you find that you have allowed a thug into your border. Mistakes do happen. I am unable to recommend the plume poppy, *Macleaya microcarpa* 'Coral Plume', for example, as its invasiveness is such as to have put the Golden Horde to shame. This is an instance of a much-perpetuated mistake in naming which has destroyed the good reputation of a first-class garden plant. *M. cordata* is a perfectly well-behaved plant that would grace any border, but its name has been given in catalogues to 'Coral Plume'. This is a shame, as 'Coral Plume' has a place in larger gardens among shrubs as a foliage plant, but nobody trusts it, while the true *M. cordata* is only seldom to be found.

Having sorted out your rear-echelon plants should leave you with a rather uneven, wavy line demarcating them from those that will be further forward. This is the time to decide whether you want to make a feature of a group of plants in such a way that they break ranks, as it were. Such a planting might take the form of a stand of delphiniums imposing order on the border by being planted in a rectangular block in a central position and occupying, not only the back rank, but also one or two of those towards the front. The dark blue variety 'Cristella', represented by a dozen plants, might be flanked by the light blue 'Loch Leven', six on each side, and then by 'Moonbeam', making a white ribbon to finish off the arrangement. Ideas such as this come readily during the planning stage, but they are impossible if you are impulsive about the whole thing.

Impulsiveness is something that can lead us into avenues which might suppress our own individuality. It is accepted by almost everyone that the border plans, both as to their colour and plant content, that were made by Gertrude Jekyll are unsurpassable. Most people arrive at this conclusion by no process of analysis. Indeed, I am not aware of that many who have ever opened one of her books, let alone studied her plans in some detail. It has just become a knee-jerk response to say 'Of course Gertrude Jekyll can never be bettered' and then to pursue patterns of pastel colours and eschew anything that is strong in hue.

In fact, Miss Jekyll was wont to include the fiercest oranges, the most demonic reds, and the strongest yellows in her designs. What she did not do was to allow them to clash shriekingly, but to graduate, via quieter tones, towards points where their natures could take the transition to other aspects of the palette. Those who ascribe to her the wishy-washy, safe pastel range are missing the whole point of her undoubted genius and would do well to study her actual plans. In them they would find some plant selections that nobody would make today. She was, for example, very fond of recommending *Elymus arenarius*, an admittedly lovely, blue-grey grass of 4 ft (1.2 m) in height, but anyone planting it would find it to be one of the greatest of all vegetable pests, rivalling some of the more invasive bamboos, and making couch grass seem like a botanical pussy-cat. Her plant choices were repetitive and rather limited, and some of the plans she drew up for clients were rather reminiscent of Mozart, whose first Flute Concerto was written by quickly transposing his Oboe Concerto note for note before he took the money and ran.

We should all feel free to express ourselves in our gardens in the ways that give us the most pleasure, and we should feel that we are at liberty to ignore the reflexes that tend to make us impulsively accept the conventional wisdoms. Just because others hate mephistophelean reds and flaming oranges should not influence our personal creativity. We should, too, make up our own minds about plants and grow them, whether they be fashionable or not, if they give us pleasure. We will certainly make mistakes, but they will be our very own and we shall learn from them.

An Example

I should be very upset indeed if I were to think that everyone would agree with my ideas about planting up a herbaceous border. It would fatally undermine my feeling that what makes the human race interesting is the infinite variety of its members and of their ways of looking at things. Similarly, I should feel that I had done very badly if any ideas of my own that I were to share with others were followed slavishly. The function of a gardening communicator should be to promote thought and not to stultify it.

Accordingly, Plan 1 should be looked at merely as an example of what can be done with a perfectly simple, small border fronting a wall of anything over 7 ft (2.1 m) in height. While you may not like the arrangement of colours others will, and thank heaven for the difference. The main thing is that as a planting it works and it does so because it has form and colour balance.

It is based, simply enough, on height at the back, but the plants will slope sharply down to the front because the border is a narrow one. In such a narrow border the plants must be packed in as tightly as possible consistent with their healthy development, otherwise a graduation of the heights of the plants is impossible – they will be either all of the same height or will consist of tall ones at the back and incongruously short ones at the front. Tight planting will have the effect of making the border look wider; larger, looser planting has the opposite effect.

The way in which the heights of the plants are arranged gives the border its form, but only in part. The shapes and styles of the foliage and flowers have to be taken into consideration, but are best looked at after the colours have been mapped out.

Plan 1 uses colour fairly loosely. Although there are blocks of similar tones (such as the yellows of *Solidago* 'Lemore', *Helichrysum* 'Sulphur Light', and *Achillea* 'Coronation Gold'), the border needs an injection of discipline if it is to be 'held together' in an orderly way. This is done in this case by using plants on three axes.

The first two axes comprise a pair, running at complementary but opposite angles through the border. They consist of plants with white flowers, whose distribu-

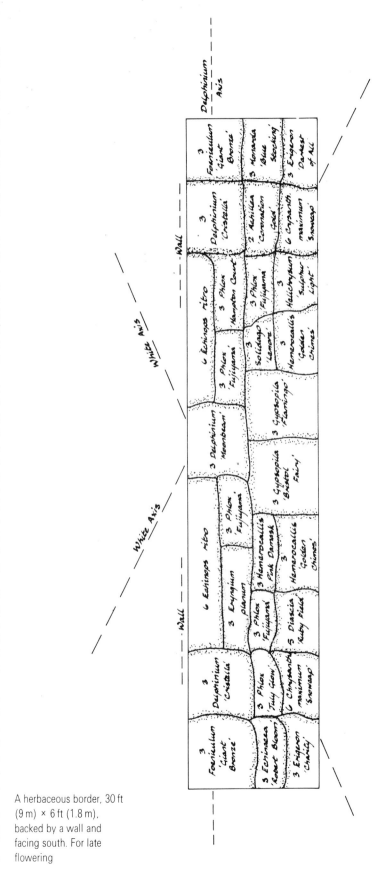

A herbaceous border, 30 ft (9 m) × 6 ft (1.8 m), backed by a wall and facing south. For late flowering

Delphinium 'Cristella'
(JH)

tion is repeated from one axis to another but with a small irregularity introduced to avoid a geometrical appearance which might have its place in a carpet bedding arrangement but not in a small herbaceous border. *Phlox* 'Fujiyama', a plant of medium height, is used in the middle, while *Chrysanthemum maximum* 'Snowcap', which has short flower stems, is placed at the front.

White is of the greatest possible value, as it separates colours from one another that might otherwise clash. In the plan, this happens where *Diascia* 'Ruby Field',

whose flowers are of a rich rose pink, is separated from *Erigeron* 'Charity' by the little chrysanthemum. The light pink of the erigeron has a bluish overlay that the diascia could not live with; the intervention of white cuts out the problem.

Of course, the use of white as a buffer is often the refuge of those who are not very good with colours. Miss Jekyll did not need to descend to such a device, although she used it when she wished to. The nearby transition, *Diascia* 'Ruby Field' – *Phlox* 'July Glow' – *Erigeron* 'Charity', works, as the phlox acts as a bridge, being clear

enough to live with the diascia, but having that hint of blue in its pink that sets up the erigeron. The switch to the purplish red of *Echinacea* 'Robert Bloom' is then a natural one, especially as it is found in front of the deep purple foliage of the fennel against the wall.

White is, then, a colour to be used quite sparingly. There is nothing to be ashamed of in using it as a buffer. I am no Renoir and therefore find it useful, but you should not surrender to the temptation to get out of trouble by using white. The thing is never to paint yourself into a corner in the first place and this means keeping a broad view of the developing border at all times, from planning to planting.

That Plan 1 is no more than an example should become crystal clear when it is pointed out that someone who is good with colours should be able to design a border of similar size without using white at all and still impose order. There are many different ways of achieving a harmonious arrangement – an element of order will come into them all – but it is the principle that matters, not the method of execution.

Phlox paniculata 'Snow Hare' – one of several varieties of a species whose best forms are probably the white ones (*JH*)

The third axis runs right from one side of the border to the other. It consists, in a border designed for late colour, of two components, delphiniums and *Echinops ritro*. During the early part of the summer, two different blues will be present in the delphiniums and they will dominate the border, encouraged by a white. The white is at the centre back of the border and, while it is present, it forms the crossing, or merging point of the two white axes. It is, therefore doing two jobs, its other being to be part of the delphinium axis of tall, stately flower spikes. *Delphinium* 'Cristella' and *D.* 'Loch Leven' are two of the most sumptuous blues, the one a little deeper than the other, and it must be said that every effort should be made to obtain named varieties, as their colours are far superior to those found in seed strains.

When the delphiniums are over and summer reaches the stage at which the garden becomes shrill with the sounds of those released from school (and even the birds hide), the blue is taken over, although in a more muted manner, by the tall, thistle-like, *Echinops ritro*. This is a fine plant, no stranger to stateliness, which grows far above the 4 to 5 ft (1.2–1.5 m) that catalogues would have us believe. In a good soil with adequate rain it can reach 7 ft (2.1 m). It provides rounded seed-heads well into the autumn, so is an ideal candidate for the job it is called upon to do. If a plant of lesser height is wanted, then the blue sea-holly, *Eryngium planum* may be called upon. Its flowering season is even longer, and it supplies an electric blue that is unique among border plants. If it flowers while the delphiniums are still out it does not matter, as it makes no clash and hides its light modestly until its turn comes to play a major part. In combination with yellow or buff day lilies (*Hemerocallis*) it is unbeatable.

While a border may be laced through with systems of order, true bilateral symmetry is boring. Plan 1 shows similarities between its two halves, right and left, and there are symmetrical elements, but the principle of avoiding a mathematical sameness between parts of the border is one that applies not only to borders of this kind, but to a lesser degree to beds and to an equal degree to mixed borders.

The habits of the plants, which is to say their ways of holding themselves, their stature (which is not the same thing as their heights), their densities of foliage, and so on, are important to the overall look of the border. It is not possible to plan for such things unless you are familiar with the plants, so it pays to do a little snooping if you are a relative beginner and to go and see other peoples' gardens whenever possible.

Do, on the other hand, try to learn something about those plants whose foliage will play a major part, as their inclusion can be most telling. Our plan juxtaposes the upright, iris-like leaves of *Hemerocallis* 'Golden Chimes' (a later flowering plant than *H. flava*, but similar if a little darker in colour) with the insubstantial, airy cloud of *Gypsophila* 'Bristol Fairy' on the one hand and *G.* 'Flamingo' on the other. Such contrasts add greatly to the quality of a planting, and can be used to enhance the effects of neighbouring flower-masses.

Planting and Care

Planting a herbaceous border is an entirely different matter from almost any other sort of planting. It is not that the actual putting of the plants in the soil is any different; the principles governing the operation are much the same for anything. It is the timing that makes the setting-up of a herbaceous border a thing apart.

It is perfectly possible for a border to be planted up a bit at a time as plants become available or mature from seed or cuttings. The gaps can be filled with annuals and the whole can be allowed to develop gradually. In practice, this tends to take years longer than was originally envisaged and what happens then is that the original plan is never carried out. If planning and preparation are to bear fruit in the shape of the herbaceous border that you really want, then you are better planting everything at once. Failing this, as much as possible should be done at the beginning.

The little bits of root that come to you from the open ground in the nursery should not put you off. They are often much sturdier plants than those that you can buy in pots and, put into the ground when dormant, they get a flying start in the spring. Herbaceous plants can be bought in pots, of course, but you can find yourself paying a high price for a lot of top growth and a sadly restricted root system. Roots are everything with herbaceous plants because they are the winter stores of nutrients and because only a good, strong root can initiate and support that fast-growing foliage and flowers.

The temptation to plant more to the square yard or metre than you know to be right because your less rational self tells you that such little things can never cover the area must be resisted. What must also be eschewed are the inevitable blandishments of fellow gardeners who, having heard of your undertaking, flock to your garden bearing dubious offerings in even more doubtful bags. The trouble with these is that they can only be refused by those versed in diplomacy at its most sophisticated. It is much better to accept with apparent glee. This will save the situation in the short term and give you time to prepare alibis for the plants which you have meanwhile consigned to the compost heap.

Much has been written of the legendary generosity of gardeners, and some of it is true. There is also a fearful snobbery attached in some cases to the giving away of plants, the dreaded sign of which is the dropping of a name of which you have never heard. 'I had it from so-and-so', goes the formula, usually suffixed by something like, 'He tells me it is the true form, not the subspecies from Albania with the two whiskers on the calyx'. Be duly wary of such pronouncements. They usually mean that the plant in question will emerge from its winter sleep not merely as a member of the wrong species but as part of an entirely different genus.

With shrubs this is not a great danger. Once the offending plant has shown itself as a usurper, it can be dug up and got rid of. With perennials, though, the giving away of wrongly-named plants, or of plants whose habits have not been explained to the recipients, can be most damaging.

A piece of the beautiful grass, *Glyceria maxima* 'Variegata', lovely in its stripes of green and yellow, might seem a fine gift, and so it would be if the giver gave strict instructions that it must be grown in dry soils if it is to remain compact. What is more likely to happen is that no such advice will be given and that the conventional wisdom that decrees a damp place for it will be followed. That the plant has invasive proclivities that Attila the Hun might envy will all too soon become apparent

Incorrect naming is all too prevalent. It is not always the fault of well-meaning, decent amateur gardeners either. The trade has cause to be ashamed of itself on occasion, too, as in the case of *Macleaya microcarpa* 'Coral Plume' cited earlier. The lesson is that you should take nobody's word about plants (not even mine) until you have done your research and satisfied yourself that you are not introducing botanical cuckoos.

Herbaceous borders have fallen out of favour with many gardeners and are no longer thought of as desirable in large gardens where labour is employed. In order that gardens of large size can be kept going at all, every device for saving labour has to be taken advantage of and those kinds of gardening that are labour-intensive have to go. Unfortunately, misconceptions about herbaceous borders have led to exaggerated ideas of their labour costs.

Traditionally, such borders have been emptied every three years, re-dug and re-manured, while the plants have been split up and the young pieces planted so as to renew the border. This is a formidable task which depends on there being a large enough labour force to get the job done on those few days that present themselves in the autumn and early winter when conditions are suitable. We no longer see the necessity for such an operation, as it can be done piecemeal as each plant or set of plants becomes due for renewal, but we still tend to the view that herbaceous borders are over-consumers of labour. Why this should concern the home gardener is difficult to see. He or she does not have to cost the labour expended on the garden and, after all, people actually like to work at gardening and are even heard to describe it as a leisure activity – what plain English prefers to call a hobby. The activities of renovating, weeding and staking are things that can be enjoyed.

Staking has suddenly become the villain of the piece. Gardeners who will spend untold hours in erecting wigwams for their runner beans of which any Blackfoot or Pawnee would have been proud, and whose peas scramble over woody confections that might rival Beecher's Brook, regard staking perennials as something to be avoided like the plague. Short perennials are sold under catalogue descriptions that laud their ability to grow without

Eryngium alpinum, one of
the blue sea-hollies and
the largest in flower (*TB*)

stakes, and remarks about 'Great ugly stakes and yards of string' abound among those who have taken up alpines. Staked early enough in the season, herbaceous perennials will soon grow up to hide their supports. Without staking, many will collapse and their flowering stems snap, so it is an essential job, but it is by no means a formidable one. It is necessary, too, for a great many of the short ones that are supposed not to need stakes. Height is relative in perennials. A catalogue description, made in good faith, of a plant that will be 4 ft (1.2 m) in height at flowering, may seem ridiculously misleading when a wet, warm summer and liberal amounts of manure induce a height of 7 ft (2.1 m) or more. Similarly, a much-vaunted 3 ft (1 m) one may be found to be twice the height before crashing to the ground one windy night.

There are several kinds of staking devices that can be obtained. They are nearly all wildly expensive and are not at all conducive to the popularity of the growing of perennials. I use bamboo canes and string – just about the cheapest method I can think of – and the ladies who maintain my 200 sq. yd (sq. m.) of herbaceous borders like it, so it must be all right.

Perennials are subject to very few diseases and to even fewer pests. This is, no doubt, a sweeping statement to make, but it is true for well-grown plants in the British Isles. The USA is full of health hazards for plants but here we may be sure that good cultivation and plenty of food will produce healthy plants. Indeed, it is safe to advise that any sick plants should be pulled up and burnt and that anything that fails two years running should be forgotten and something else put in its place.

There will always be years when attacks by aphids become unacceptable and when leaf-rollers and leaf-miners take hold. A systemic insecticide will take care of almost everything in this line and it will not have to be repeated very often, unlike contact sprays, whose use has to be so frequent that it becomes a bore. Even in such years, however, well-grown plants will shrug off infestations, even if they are quite severe.

The insect that perennials cannot tolerate is the ant. If the soil is left a bit puffy, or there are large lumps, between which are passages that are like motorways to

small insects, the ants will invade and make their nests. They will usually be red ants, which is all the more uncomfortable for the gardener, and they will cause havoc among the roots of the plants. For some reason they seem to like living with *Papaver orientale* cultivars. If you see these turn burnt-looking and collapsed, ants will very likely be the cause.

Perennials become less effective as each plant ages. Ageing is not easy to understand. On the face of it, a plant has a finite lifespan. That of a shrub may be anything from seven years or thereabouts to many decades, while a perennial will be old and decrepit at seven. What makes the concept of plant age complicated is what happens when we clone a plant. Take a piece off an elderly plant and it will be young once it grows its own roots or accepts, as in peonies, the roots of the plants onto which it is grafted. A cutting from a 100-year-old camellia starts off as if it were a 10-year-old (but note, not a yearling), and a division of a border phlox has all the vigour of youth that the parent plant had begun to lose.

Nothing living is immortal, however. Ageing is merely slowed down by the cloning process; it is not eliminated. Every clone becomes progressively weaker as it is propagated, and this is why some of the plants that were well-known in gardens in the 1920s have now disappeared and some of Miss Jekyll's designs can no longer be carried out without looking for substitutes.

Perennials are shorter-lived as plants and as clones than woody plants. They need to be propagated more often, thereby becoming weaker and the occurrence of viruses weakens the stocks even more. To raise new ones is a constant pursuit of nurserymen and plant breeders, and it behoves us to renew our species (but not our cultivars) from seed occasionally. Meanwhile, we need to divide our plants regularly, but not slavishly.

Propagation details are given elsewhere, but it is worth mentioning that the outer parts of a plant are the ones that, detached, will exhibit youthfulness. The old, middle bit should be thrown away.

The herbaceous border that is properly planned and that has been planted up more or less at one time will be a constant source of new plants, not only for its own replanting, but also as a surplus. What you do with the surplus is up to you. You can preside over an ever increasing family of herbaceous borders, or you can give them away to somebody who is making one for themselves.

Whatever you do, allow them a way of refusing, and when you come to see their borders when they have reached maturity, do not make the mistake of asking after your erstwhile children. They will probably be on the compost heap.

Two activities that are cited as further prohibitive factors in the labour needed for a herbaceous border are dead-heading and cutting-back. Dead-heading is a fiddly job, one of those that sends you daft with boredom because the brain is forced to run in neutral, while cutting-back is an annual chore that involves the satisfaction of the restoration of neatness. It also stimulates thought, usually of the planning kind.

It is much better to combine the two activities into one large job that may be spread over a week or two, depending on the size of your border and the varieties of plants. There is, of course, nothing to stop you indolently tweaking the odd spent flower head from its mooring as you pass by on a warm evening, but it is a counsel of perfection that dead-heading should be carried out in the full sense. Besides, it is all too likely that, as your mind freewheels its way through the odd thoughts that take your fancy, you will find that you have destroyed the whole crop of some highly valued seed.

Cutting-back is essential, of course, otherwise the whole bed will eventually become a horticultural *Marie Celeste*. Some things, notably forms of *Papaver orientale*, become very untidy in high summer, and benefit from being cut back so that just a small proportion of their leaf area is left. New leaves will follow, to die down in their turn later, but they will be small. Most other plants, however, become candidates for being cut back from about the middle of August but can be left quite satisfactorily until later.

If you are in any doubt about when to cut back, then a simple rule should solve the problem. The flowering stems of most perennials (but by no means all) emerge from clumps, or rosettes, of foliage. These elongate as the stems lengthen and you will find that the plants consist almost entirely of flowering stems, each with leaves along its length. Some time after flowering,

secondary rosettes of foliage will appear at the bases of the plants and it is when this happens that you can feel perfectly safe in cutting back the old stems.

Whether you leave the whole job of cutting back until October or tackle it gently a bit at a time will have a lot to do with your own particular standards of neatness and the way in which you like to work. There are no hard and fast rules, but one should always bear in mind that the plants are our greatest teachers and that observation is a great asset in a gardener.

Mixed Borders

Whatever we may think about the future of the herbaceous border, we cannot deny that the day of the small garden is with us to stay. As, happily, more and more people come to own gardens – and most of them are small – so the force of the gardening communicator's message must be increasingly directed towards and influenced by those who garden on a small scale.

The small garden has little room for herbaceous borders because it would be achingly empty for such a long time. Whereas a large garden will contain other colourful elements that will make the seasonal bareness of the herbaceous border less noticeable, the small gardener must resort to a different kind of gardening. Among the available options is the relatively modern one of the mixed border.

It is not just the desire to avoid a negative that makes for the use of mixed borders. Those who do not have a great deal of space and who are keen on plants will want to grow as many of their favourites as they can. To segregate them into separate quarters is possible, again, in large gardens, but in small ones it is not a practical proposition. The mixed border has grown out of the innate plantsmanship that is in people at large, as well as out of the exigencies of modern living.

Paradoxically, those whose gardening horizons are not so limited are now as keen on the idea as anyone else. You are quite likely to visit one of the great gardens that are open to the public and to find that many of the older, more formal plantings have given way to the apparently more casual, mixed ones. That the casualness is

Left: A little time spent staking *Echinacea purpurea* is surely worthwhile (*TB*)

Right: Don't be too keen to dead-head everything in sight. Some plants, like *Agapanthus*, need to be grown from seed (*JH*)

more apparent than real is something that will become more clear as an understanding of the principles underlying mixed borders grows.

The inhabitants of a mixed border will be very different in their natures. While some will have lifespans of several decades, others can only be expected to live for three or four years before they will need to be refurbished. While the whole border will be in sun (for we are still talking about perennials in sun) some thought will have to be given to the incidence of shade as the more long-lived plants grow larger. A mixed border is just what it says – a mixture of small trees with shrubs, bulbs and perennials and, unlike the herbaceous border, whose pattern and identity are established early and need never change. Instead it grows year by year, passing through a childhood, adolescence, and into an adulthood.

Preparation of the ground need be no different. Indeed, there is no substitute for the old-fashioned ingredient of hard work. If you get it right from the start the plants will reward you by being strong, lush and able to repel and shake off diseases and pests. They may very well be more winter hardy, too, and you will have saved yourself a great deal more work and expense in the long run. It is hard to imagine shrubs growing harmoniously with perennials if one party or another is existing on shorter commons than its fellow. Consider the border as a whole as far as preparation goes and only then think about what will go where. That way you will not condemn some deserving plant to a struggle on a left-out bit of soil, neither will you have cosseted the perennials at the expense of the woody plants.

Choosing and Planning

The choice of plants and the ways in which they are used might seem to be obvious. We are creating a mixed border. We know how to make a herbaceous border. So why not just mix shrubs and herbaceous plants together? What could be more simple?

If that were all there was to it I should be out of a job. Gardening is not a complicated business, but it is not a pastime for duffers either. The reason why I am gainfully employed is that gardening well is within the reach of everyone but the logic behind it is, though simple, obscured by woolly thinking on the one hand and professional obscurantism on the other. My function is to explain. In the case of mixed borders, the explanation has to do with the inescapable fact that a very high proportion of them end up as tree and shrub borders. This is because of the almost universal impatience that governs our lives. We must have instant effects or suffer a jittery agony of unfulfilment. Nowhere is this more so than with gardening. The gardener who fills his garden with annuals bypasses this feeling, and so does the one who wishes to garden exclusively with perennials. Bring on the trees and shrubs, though, and all sense flies through the window.

This is not a book about woody plants, but it is nowadays impossible to discuss fully any group of plants in a garden context without involving some recognition of the others. A mixed border is one of the homes for perennials in the garden and they will be intimately affected by their woody neighbours. What must be avoided at all costs is their being terminally affected – a fate that awaits them in the gardens of the impatient.

Shrubs and trees, bought at a nursery in quite small pots, do not impress greatly when put in the ground, especially as their apparent heights will be considerably less than when they stood free in the sales beds in their pots. The temptation to plant too many too closely together is overwhelming, especially as it is not always easy in modern garden sales establishments to obtain knowledgeable advice as to the ultimate heights and spreads of the plants.

The result is that after a very few years the garden sports a superabundance of trees and shrubs which have either to be pruned in an increasingly severe and damaging way, or which have to be moved to other parts of the garden. Eventually there is nowhere left to move them and the garden becomes their exclusive domain, save for a few flowers, crushed between shrubs and lawn, sadly trying to give summer cheer amid the encircling green. A respect for and understanding of the plants will achieve balance and harmony, but it will take a balanced and harmonious spirit to achieve such feelings.

I know a garden which is quite large. It contains two long, parallel mixed borders which were lovely for a few years. Phloxes and campanulas lent their summery colours in drifts, while carpets of *Dianthus* suggested the scents and sights of the cottage garden. There were shrubs too, forming a strong backbone to each border and bringing blazes of colour in the spring and early summer in company with bulbs. Trees, seemingly well spaced, and certainly not of the sort that would eventually become too large, gave height and architectural point to the plantings. Now, however, the shrubs reach out and lay claim to the whole area except for little pockets in which a few perennials grasp at a tenuous existence. So few are they that after the shrubs have done flowering there is little colour in what were once joyous borders. Most shrubs are spring-flowering, with the month of May as the apogee of their effort. After that it is other things that give the greater part of the colour in a garden and here they have been crowded out. In losing the balance of harmony between the groups of plants the spread of colour through the season has been lost too.

If the owner of the garden had taken note of what the shrubs would be like a few years after planting and had not wanted to achieve the desired effect too quickly, the borders would by now have been approaching adulthood, having passed through the exuberance and greed of adolescence. *Chrysanthemum coccineum (Pyrethrum roseum)* 'Brenda', whose bright red flowers are among those that take over the roles of some of the brasher shrubs of spring as summer gets under way, would be being given free rein, instead of languishing palely, barely able to thrust a complaining bloom heavenwards through a tangle of berberis.

Trees must be chosen for size, of course. It goes without saying that you would not plant oaks in a mixed border, but this example is rendered ludicrous only because it is extreme. Your choice will be a matter of degree, and you are likely to look for varieties of *Sorbus aucuparia* (the mountain ashes), crab apples, or some of the smaller (but not smallest) species of *Acer*. What I fear you are all too likely to do is to spend an unwarranted fortune on specimens that are far too large and which are unlikely ever to become wind-firm, or to buy and plant too many.

Smaller specimens usually catch up and pass larger ones because their root systems are larger in comparison with their amount of foliage and they have not spent some years in striving merely to exist. Furthermore, because their anchoring roots can get thoroughly set before their heads get up into the wind (winds are a great deal weaker near the ground than a few feet above it), they are less likely to blow over at an age when their loss and the damage they cause in falling is an embarrassment. To plant too many is the besetting sin, leading to sterility of the environment for other plants and to one's having borders that are nothing more than stands of small trees.

Similar considerations govern the choice of shrubs, and it must be noted that there are not very many shrubs that are small. It is all too tempting to pick up a lovely, bushy specimen of, say, *Photinia* 'Red Robin' and to bear it away imagining its rich, red new growths and its ability to grow on your calcareous soil. Planted, it will give you a moment of doubt about your investment. It will look so small and lonely, surrounded by the tall, arrogant spires of delphiniums, stately red-hot pokers like 'Atlanta', or Russell lupins. Give it just a few years, however, and it will make refugees of the tallest perennials, banishing them as travellers, gift-wrapped for a neighbour's garden.

Practical aspects of another sort are involved in the management of a mixed border. Care must be taken that shrubs that are sensitive in their roots are not allowed to take too enthusiastic a part. Magnolias, particularly the small ones of the *M. stellata* persuasion, are just what one would call to mind after the strictures that apply to size have been realised. Indeed, they are worthy members of the mixed border, but their place is where there will be no digging and delving within their root areas. Any disturbance of the roots of a magnolia sets it back badly, sometimes fatally, so it is best to allow it plenty of uncluttered space in which to develop. It will reward you in the end by clothing itself to the ground with foliage and flowers if it is one of the smaller ones (the larger magnolias are ultimately very large) and will, as a result of your patience, look completely at home among its perennial neighbours.

Chrysanthemum coccineum 'Brenda' (*JH*)

Penstemon 'Cherry', whose bright flowers are all the better against the greens of surrounding shrubs (*JH*)

Left: A well-balanced mixed border in which there is interest in foliage or flowers for the greater part of the year (*JK*)

Rosa moyesii 'Geranium'

Clematis 'Jackmanii' and
Hedera colchica 'Paddy's Pride'

Sambucus
racemosa
'Plumosa Aurea'

6 Blue
Delphiniums
6 White Jap
anemones

X Osmarea
burkwoodii

Sorbus
cashmiriana

6 Echinops ritro
10 Digitalis Mertonensis

3 Hosta
'Honeybells'

3 Hosta
'Royal
Standard'

Malus
'Red
Jade'

Rose
Fru Dagmar
Hastrup
(pruned)

6
Penstemon
'Garnet'

3 Diascia
rigescens

8 Schizostylis
'Mrs Hegarty'

Hebe
rakaiensis

3 Lamium maculatum
'Beacon Silver'
3 Potentilla 'Gibsons
Scarlet'

Clematis montana

Choisya
ternata

Lilies

3 Eryngium
variifolium

3 Paeonia
Sarah
Bernhardt

Acer
griseum

8 Bergenia
schmidtii

Hedera helix 'Buttercup'

8 Pink Japanese
anemones

8 Malva
moschata
alba

6 Potentilla
nepalensis
'Roxana'

N

A mixed border, 30 ft
(9 m) × 9 ft (2.7 m) and
24 ft (7.2 m) × 9 ft
(2.7 m), backed by walls.
Soil: alkaline

An Example

Plan 2 represents a mixed border made on the angle formed by two walls of around 9 ft (2.7 m) in a reasonably small urban garden. The climate is one in which hard frosts are fairly frequent and whose summers are uninspiring. The soil is moderately alkaline but it has been well and thoroughly prepared and manured. It is, in short, about as ordinary a situation as you could imagine.

Exactly the same sentiments apply to it as did to the plan for a herbaceous border on p. 31. I do not delude myself that anyone is going to go out and attempt to execute it (although that would be very flattering); neither would I be at all happy if there were not a large number of gardeners who disagreed with its contents and dispositions. We would be reduced to the status of zombies if we all went about things the same way, but we are logical creatures, able to appreciate the general principles that underlie a particular example. The shrubs and trees have been chosen to provide interest at different times of the year. In the corner of the two walls is the golden cut-leaved elder, *Sambucus racemosa* 'Plumosa Aurea', whose golden foliage will dominate from spring to autumn. Spring will see its flat heads of yellowish-white flowers while, in a good year, there should be an abundant crop of scarlet berries in the summer. The rest of the planting is planned outwards from this shrub.

It is probably as good a way as any other of planning a mixed border to decide on one dominant feature and then to let everything flow from that. You will find that relationships between the plants are easy to work out because the plants themselves dictate them. For instance, the gold of the elder demands that its flanking neighbours should be of a clear, dark green, one that will make a clear contrast. A light green, or one that had yellow in it, would suffer by comparison. *Osmarea burkwoodii* (now corrected to *Osmanthus* 'Burkwoodii') and *Choisya ternata* both qualify in this respect. These two shrubs are also unlikely to attain sizes that will become an embarrassment and lead to the mixed borders becoming merely another shrubbery. The amount of space allocated to them and to the other trees and shrubs is pretty realistic, as far as one can be allowed to generalise about different rates of growth in a variety of situations. That is why there are so few woody plants in the plan; any more and overcrowding would ensue with the onset of maturity.

The choisya and the osmarea are evergreens. This quality allows them to play another role; that of winter decoration. Their presence, one on either side of the corner, provides structure and is echoed by the low-growing, olive-green hump of *Hebe rakaiensis* at the front of the longer arm of the border. As it is set out, there is no corresponding evergreen shrub accent on the shorter arm, but this is an option that could be fulfilled by something like one of the smaller kinds of evergreen berberis like *B. bristolensis*.

There are three trees, all of which qualify for that modern category 'Ideal for The Small Garden'. Sometimes I think that if I hear once more about The Small Garden I shall become a gibbering wreck. Still, most gardens are small and there it is. However, that is no excuse for the situation that arises wherein only a small range of trees can be bought at the main retail outlets. It is even less reason why those whose business it is to recommend plants should be confined to the straitjacket of what is readily available. If you do not hear about plants that are a bit more unusual how are you going to create the 'call' for them that you are always told does not exist?

Sorbus cashmiriana is the perfect companion tree for perennials. Its light, pinnate foliage does not create a deep shade, and its white berries last right into the winter, long after the perennials have finished. Of course, the garden centres will tell you that there is only a 'call' for red-berried mountain ashes. Maybe so. What we should be doing is demanding the white-berried sorts because the red berries are eaten by birds before we have a chance to appreciate them.

Acer griseum is a different kettle of fish. This wonderful small tree, whose mahogany bark peels so that papery flakes of it catch the sun with a deep orange glow, is difficult to propagate. It can only be grown from seed in the normal way of things, and it is reluctant to germinate. However, demand has dictated that the ingenuity of the propagator be stretched a bit, and the tree is becoming more easy to obtain.

The well known *Malus* 'Red Jade' is in the plan for the architectural shape of its weeping branches, as well as for its flowers and fruit. The bare branches of deciduous woody plants are important elements in the attractiveness of the border in winter, and they should be chosen with this in mind. As it is, our plan provides this characteristic, as well as contrasting foliage, evergreen interest, berries, flowers, and pretty bark. Not bad for a Small Garden!

No gardener worth the name would be seen dead with bare walls, and our plan reflects this. There is nothing ultra-sophisticated about the planting on the walls. The bright yellow variegation of *Hedera colchica* 'Paddy's Pride' will be stunningly combined with *Clematis* 'Jackmanii' in late summer, and the *Hedera/Clematis* connection is carried out on the other wall, but in a different way. *Rosa moyesii* 'Geranium' seems alone and a little out of things, but this is not so; its magnificent, light red hips, large and like upturned amphorae, are answered by the equally large, round, tomato-like ones on the rugosa rose 'Fru Dagmar Hastrup', kept low by pruning, that occupies the crucial junction between the two arms of the border.

It is the trees and shrubs with their armoury of interest throughout the year that dictate order and theme to the border. The perennials in a mixed border must come second in design terms as, for the most part, they are temporary actors in the year's events. It is, therefore, fruitless to attempt to use the same sorts of design ideas and principles that applied in the herbaceous border. There is, too, a certain informality about a mixed border, whereas a herbaceous border cannot escape from

Diascia rigescens and *Malva moschata* 'Alba' (*TB*)

Helleborus foetidus is an evergreen perennial (*JH*)

Above: Geum 'Mrs Bradshaw' (*JH*)

Left: Sensible spacing at Barnsdale. Geoff Hamilton's mixed border is unlikely to become crowded (*JK*)

formalisation of design without becoming a jumble or, in the hands of an expert, a cottage-garden planting.

Just as it seems a good idea to start planning on the basis of the positioning of one major tree or shrub, so it is from the woody plants that we should allow design with the perennials to come. There are two ways of looking at this. On the one hand, you can look at, say, *Choisya ternata*, whose glossy, dark green, trifoliolate foliage and scented, white flowers make it such a favourite, and you can think to yourself that a white phlox might be just the job in front of it, as it would carry on when the flowers of the shrub had finished. On the other hand, you might wish to find a home for the bright red *Penstemon utahensis* that you have grown from seed from a friend in the United States of America. You think that the dark green leaves will set it off beautifully and you plant it there. The first approach is design-oriented, while the latter is the approach of the plantsman.

The essential difference between the two is that the design-oriented gardener tends to try to find plants that will fit into the plan that is developing – 'I need a sulphur yellow just here' – while the pure plantsman looks for a place where his plant will be happy, no matter what sort of a mishmash it may cause in terms of design, although luck and a certain unconscious artistic bent may come into play from time to time. When the plantsman grows up and gets beyond the mere making of a collection is when he adopts the attitude of design-orientation and applies his plantsmanship to it. Here, the next step is to think of what will go happily alongside the bright red penstemon and it might be that something like the pink *Diascia rigescens* will be chosen.

Be that as it may, our plan asks that the choisya should act as a foil for the highly ornamental sea-holly, *Eryngium variifolium*. This has rosettes of spiny leaves with strikingly marked white veins. The flowers have wide, white collars and are bluish-grey. The stems are not very tall, but they are taller than the foliage of the peony in front which will, when it goes down for the winter, reveal the sea-holly foliage for us to see clearly, for it is evergreen.

The reason why we did not include another evergreen shrub (such as the berberis suggested as an alternative option

earlier) becomes clear when we see that the plan brings together the sea holly and a substantial group of a bergenia. It need not necessarily be *Bergenia schmidtii*; this is just one among many that will do just as well. It is, perhaps, not as showy in its flowers as others, but it has nice, toothed leaves that are unfailingly of a fresh, light green.

There are not that many evergreen perennials that they should be forgotten. Conversely, when they are used, their evergreen natures are often overlooked so that they are not properly exploited for creating interest in the mixed border during the colder weather. Among the more useful are such plants as *Anthemis cupaniana*, whose silver-grey foliage is a permanent feature in the milder counties, the lavender-blue *Campanula latiloba*, and its near-relative, *C. persicifolia*. This last will turn out to be a good, reliable, evergreen perennial with interestingly long, narrow leaves as long as it is obtained simply as the species or as a strain such as Peach Bells. It is grown from seed which will give plants of varying shades of blue with an occasional white, so you might be better off sowing it yourself if you want a particular shade.

Many hellebores are evergreen and, although they are discussed among the perennials in shade, some of their number are happy in a moisture-retentive soil in sun. Euphorbias, on the other hand, tend to like all the sun that they can get, while retaining a degree of toleration of shade. Other genera among which evergreen perennials can be sought are *Phormium, Kniphofia, Pulmonaria, Sisyrinchium, and Tellima*. Those ferns that are evergreen are, too, more suitably thought of for shade.

The long arm of the mixed border in Plan 2 is designed to look pretty over a long season with both flower and foliage interest coming into play. It has little more to tell us about the subject apart from its being more or less divided into three distinct areas, one of which is at the back with taller plants and hostas in front of them; another has a pink theme, and the third is a mixture of a ground-covering, silver-leaved plant with one bearing brilliant red flowers.

The point is that there is a flexibility and a labour-saving element to a mixed border that cannot happen in the classic herbaceous border. Whereas we have seen that the herbaceous borders are not any longer subject to regular uprootings and re-diggings, they are, if well designed, so concerned with the interlocking of plant relationships that it is not easy to disman-tle one part and recast it completely with-out destroying the overall design.

If a section of Plan 1 were to be taken up and totally new plants used to replace it, the design would, depending upon which part were reorganised, be radically changed or completely ruined. On the other hand, to remove the plants from one of the 'rooms' (such as the three discrete areas in Plan 2) that develop as a mixed border matures is to open up possibilities for adventure and fun.

This is the essential difference between a herbaceous border of the classic kind and a mixed border and it also represents the different approaches to gardening that re-flect the passing of the twentieth century. The strict formality that accompanies the herbaceous border is an essential component. The mixed border dismisses formality and opens the door to true plantsmanship, whereby form and habit, structure and character supplement the colours as they come and go. It is the plants that dominate, rather than flowers alone, and the imagination and flair of the gardener is released and allowed full rein, even within today's limited garden boundaries.

Kniphofia 'Atlanta' and Russell lupins (*JH*)

Chapter Two
Sunny Informality

The progress – if that is the word – from the formality of the herbaceous border to the relative freedom of the mixed border may seem to be in line with the way in which we think generally about things in the modern era. We consider ourselves to be totally liberated from the strictures that inhibited people in the Victorian age and beyond into the first half of the century and think that we and our American cousins invented informality.

In gardening terms, nothing could be further from the truth. While it is certainly true that a strong thread of formal arrangement has run through western gardening since its early beginning in Persia, this has mainly been confined to the rich – to those who have been able over the centuries to command sufficient capital and labour to allow of such a luxury. Informality was the keynote of the ordinary person (which is to say, for the most part, the poor) and plants were put in where they were most practically sited. Aesthetic considerations were, of course, involved. Poverty and lack of education may prevent the sophistication of aesthetic sense; they cannot destroy it, and the cottage gardens that abounded beyond the boundaries of the demesnes of the landowners were proof of this.

Beds for Perennials

One informal development that is modern, however, is the perennial bed. As we have seen earlier, flower beds, as opposed to borders, were where annuals of short stature were grown so that the eyeline across them should not be interrupted. To grow perennials in beds is, surprisingly, quite revolutionary. A bed is, unlike a border, a well-defined area of soil that does not depend for a boundary on a wall, hedge, fence, or other background structure. Its contents can be viewed from at least two sides and must, therefore be viewable from at least two sides. In other words, if you plant a bed like you would a border, you are going to find yourself rather like a bookie who finds himself faced with the view of the back of the grandstand; his rival on the other side is getting all the business because he is the one who can see the punters.

Mr Alan Bloom is credited with having invented the island bed for perennials. I cannot concur with this, but would support any claim that was made that our understanding and greatly increased use of beds as opposed to borders owe a great deal to him. An island bed is, of course, just what you would expect. The main thing about its planting, if it is to be effective, is that it should be viewable from all sides. Older gardens tended to have their beds constructed more as bridging items between borders or as extensions forward from them. Mr Bloom has certainly reminded us of what a bed is and told us a great deal about how to plant one.

However, there is no great mystery about it once you have started to think along the lines of either Plan 1 (p. 31) or Plan 2 (p. 46). In the case of the herbaceous border (Plan 1) all you do is put another one back to back with it and lo! you have a bed full of perennials and not a border. Mind you, not all that many people would make such a structure; they would be far more likely to make a mixed bed, rather like one of the arms of Plan 2 but a little wider and with, of course, no wall behind it.

The next step is merely to stop thinking about rectangles and to define beds in curves that will suit the plants that you want to put in the beds, the garden itself, the other beds that you might make, and your own personality. This is the genius of Mr Bloom's popularisation; the beds can interact with one another both as to shapes and as to contents. All this is not entirely new or modern but we may think of it as being so. It has liberated us from the stylised gardening that preceded the likes of Jekyll and has enabled us to get the most out of the gardens that we are lucky enough to be able to afford – not because of our social and economic states, but because of the bit of history that we live in.

Any informality that is to work must have rules. An Englishman who calls me Mr does so because he has been brought up to be formal. He might have no respect for me at all. An American, on the other hand, who will call me by my first name immediately, is able to use such informality because it indicates respect for the fact that I am a fellow human being. It is his rule and it structures his informality. Similarly, a bed in which perennials are to grow, with or without the company of woody plants, must be planted according to certain rules if its informality is to work. There are two principal ones. The first is that the taller plants should not obscure the shorter ones, and the other, which applies to mixed beds, is that the long-term nature of the woody plants must be taken into consideration without fail. If this is not done, the damage will be greater than in a mixed border, especially if the beds are island ones that have been made so that they are interdependent design elements. Your Pfitzer juniper that looked so appealing in its youth and about which the campanulas and day-lilies played so happily can all too soon require the attentions of a chainsaw to stop it from gobbling up the Bauhaus curve of lawn that you so artistically created between its bed and the next.

Some gardens that were originally thoroughly well designed have been ruined by this one factor alone. The greedy desire to obtain an instant effect is bad enough in any kind of gardening. Where beds are used to grow mixtures of perennials and woody plants and restraint and patience are not practised, it is inevitable that the passage of years will see the development of an overgrown mess.

Island beds are almost limitless in their capacity for providing variations on planting schemes. You may, if you have enough space, find yourself able to make one or two over purely to perennials, although it is more likely that you will include some bulbs for spring. Another might contain nothing but shrubs, while the whole complex of beds with the interposing stretches

or paths of lawn, becomes an integrated unit to the extent that you eventually stop being conscious of whether you have made beds, borders or anything else and think of your garden as a whole.

Beds, particularly island beds, have the advantage of allowing light to fall on the plants from all sides, especially if they are properly planted so that the woody components are of appropriate sizes. What is more, the plants will be subject to all the winds that blow from whatever direction. This may seem to be a distinct disadvantage but is, in fact, the reverse. The protection of a plant from wind and its protection from the action of wind are two different things. A wall or a hedge or nearby trees protect a plant from both. A stake protects it from the wind's action. Protection from the action of wind seriously weakens a plant structurally and renders it more susceptible to being damaged by the very wind from which it appears to be protected.

Experiments carried out comparatively recently have shown that plants grown under complete protection from wind in glasshouses have their wind-resisting structure significantly increased if they are shaken fairly, but not very vigorously a few times each day. Furthermore, they tend to be of shorter stature, all other things being equal. This is in line with recent work with tree-staking which has led us to stake only the lower parts of the trunks of young trees so that the roots are unable to be disturbed but the stems can sway and be induced to build up wood in an 'Eiffel Tower' pattern rather than as tubes.

Plants in borders, sheltered from some winds and deprived of some light, tend to grow tall and straight and to need staking. The light, airy environment of the open bed reduces these characters considerably and many plants that otherwise need props can be left to grow compactly and with a new-found sturdiness. While it is no argument against the herbaceous border that staking is necessary, many gardeners are sufficiently modern in their thinking to believe that if Nature does not stake plants, then neither should they.

The reverse side of the coin is that borders are necessarily self-limiting. There are only a few places in a given garden where you can put a border and you cannot go on widening it for ever; it tends to develop paths and to become a series of beds. Beds, on the other hand, are mysteriously imbued with a proclivity for reproduction that confounds sense, money, and eventually the capacity of a garden to remain designed rather than invaded.

I once lived in a house that had a large garden. It was almost entirely composed of lawn when I arrived but when I left it was as if a tide had come in, gradually engulfing the green sward with wave upon wave of heathers, alpines, shrubs, perennials and a few trees, all jostling for *Lebensraum* in a series of island beds that increased every year with the addition of 'just one more'. It was as well that I left when I did, otherwise there would have been nowhere to put that best of all garden tools, the deck-chair, and no time to sit in it in any case.

The Cottage Garden Ideal

It is tempting, in following our survey of the ways perennials can be grown in sunny positions, to think of the cottage garden as being the height of informality. This is not quite true, as it is among the situations in which perennials are grown in shade that real, naturalistic informality rules supreme. Nevertheless, the turning from formality that has led gardeners to plant mixed, instead of purely herbaceous, borders has also led them backwards, historically speaking, to the groomed jumble that is the modern version of the old cottage garden. That this is an idealised version is perfectly true, but it is none the worse for that.

It is idealistic to think that we can recreate the cottage gardens of former times because we do not live in those times and the *raisons d'être* for the cottage garden proper have gone. What we can do, though, is to marry that haphazard 'style' of gardening to the plants and the design-consciousness that our modern affluence has blessed us with.

There is a school of thought that maintains that the cottage garden should only contain those plants that would have been available to a cottager. What nonsense is this? In what era is this hypothetical cottager supposed to have lived? In the agricultural economy of the seventeenth century or in the industrial one of the late nineteenth? Would Paisley pinks and show auriculas have arrived in his garden from weavers or spinners, or would he (far more likely she) have received a slip of lavender from his aunt on the next farm? This sort of horticultural purism is all too common. That is by no means to say that a garden restricted to those plants known to Tradescant, should not be created at Hatfield, where he worked for the Cecils; it is to insist that restrictions based, not on scholarship but on nebulous, half-digested, faintly snobbish ideas are anathema to those who see them for what they are. You must, of course, be free to grow what you like, but others must not be bound by unfounded prejudices.

It is all too easy to get your history wrong, so why not plant things and relax? One person who went on and on about the historical accuracy of her cottage garden had the nerve to swank about the quality of her Russell lupins. They were, indeed, beautiful and well grown, but the Russell strain was not introduced until just before the Second World War.

To leave lupins out of the cottage garden, however, is a great pity. The Russells come in lovely, bright colours, derived from *Lupinus polyphyllus*, the Californian lupin that Steinbeck delighted in where it grew among poppies. The combination works well in cultivation, too, not with the earlier flowering *Papaver orientale* varieties, but with the lighter, smaller poppies such as *P. nudicaule*. These are usually short-lived but renew themselves from seed without being asked. The Russell strain has begun to become a little weak now, but new ones have cropped up recently in which the stems are shorter and sturdier, the flower spikes fatter and longer, and the colours clear and bold. They are worth the money that their seed costs and can be pre-germinated on wet blotting paper before being very gently potted up.

The cottage garden is not really something that you can plan. It has a Topsy-like quality if it is to be successful and it demonstrates, because its growth is gradual, the personality and character of its creator. There are no guidelines that are

Above: Geranium psilostemon 'Bressingham Fair'. Just one of the many plants with which the Bloom family have enriched gardens everywhere (*JH*)

worth mentioning; any that one might invent for the sake of sounding experienced and wise would merely be restrictive. It goes without saying that, in general, shorter plants will be placed in front of taller ones, but that is about all. The best cottage gardens are the ones that you would think were so full of plants that not one more could be squeezed in. Dense planting does away with a lot of staking, but if you have to stake, then twiggy pea-sticks are the best things to use.

The good cottage garden has about it that look that only the very best hair stylists can impart: well-groomed careless-ness. Campanulas will lean casually on neighbourly rose-bushes, pinks will rub cat-like against the ankles of sweet peas, and you have to be careful not to tread on the night-scented stock as you reach up for the loganberries. Yes, annuals have their place in the cottage garden. There is no kind of plant that does not, although each plant has its place. A plant in the wrong place is a weed.

Though I have chosen to divide the places perennials grow in into two – the sunny and the shady – it does not follow

Above: Barnsdale: the cottage garden. Modern ideas mix with old to give a variety of habitats for perennials from the very small to the statuesque (*JK*)

Right: Cottage-style planting in a shady corner (*JK*)

that they will always be at a distance from one another. Most gardens have sunny and shady places and they are often immediately next to one another. In many other kinds of gardens the style will change as the aspect dictates either sun or shade, but this does not apply in cottage gardens. This is because the style is not dependent upon the plants. The plants, wherever they are put in the cottage garden, are put in a cottagey style. It is gardeners who work in this way who often uncover chain-bred myths, such as the reputed hatred of hostas for sun or the translating of the peony's hatred for cold early summers as a loathing of shade.

Chapter 3
Plants for Sunny Places

Unless otherwise stated, the plants in this chapter prefer a good, well-prepared garden soil in sun. Only exceptional requirements are given otherwise, such as an inability to thrive on calcareous (limy) soils.

ACANTHUS Acanthaceae
—mollis
Bear's Breeches. This will grow in shade but is far better in sun, especially for flowering. The large, handsome leaves are lobed and are the ones seen modelled on Corinthian columns. Flower spikes are stiff and prickly; flowers are lilac-pink or whitish.

4 ft (1.2 m), 3 per sq. yd/m, summer.

—spinosus
Very large leaves, up to 3 ft (1 m) long distinguish this species. They are deeply lobed and have spiny points. Free-flowering, with stiff stems carrying long spikes of lilac-pink flowers. *A. spinosissimus* has leaves much like some noble, silvery thistle. It needs a lot of warmth and does not flower very well.

4 ft (1.2 m), 2 per sq. yd/m, summer, *Acanthus* species have a tendency to be invasive.

ACHILLEA Compositae
There are many garden forms of the species, with colours ranging from white through to the deepest red. Apart from yellows, of which forms of *A filipendulina* and the closely related 'Coronation Gold' are unbeatable, the new Galaxy achilleas have seen all their predecessors off. There are a handful of good varieties and there will surely soon be more. The flat flower heads of most achilleas look best when not staked and allowed to flop. *A.* 'The Pearl', however, should be staked.

Mostly 3-4 ft (1-1.2m), 3 per sq. yd/m. summer.

ACONITUM Ranunculaceae
—bicolor
This name covers most of the garden monkshoods, most of which have tall spikes of hooded, dark blue flowers in late summer, although some are bicoloured. The darkest is 'Spark's Variety', with flowers of a dusky, blackish blue, while 'Ivorine' is an early-flowering white.

4 ft (1.2 m), 4 per sq. yd/m, summer.

AGAPANTHUS Liliaceae
—Headbourne Hybrids
Agapanthus are plants that everyone wants to grow but are only successful in mild areas in the main. However, these hybrids are much hardier than the several species and are worth trying almost anywhere provided that they have full sun and a deep, rich soil. Large, terminal clusters of rich blue flowers (there are white forms) in late summer over strap-shaped leaves.

3 ft (1 m), 5-6 per sq. yd/m, late summer.

ALCHEMILLA Rosaceae
—mollis
The rounded, greyish-green leaves of this low-growing plant are covered with a down of hairs that traps drops of rain so that they shine like diamonds when the sun shines on them. The flowers are tiny and yellow-green in billowing, low clouds. They are best removed before seeding can take place, otherwise the plant will become a nuisance.

1 ft (30 cm), 6 per sq. yd/m, early summer.

ALSTROEMERIA Amaryllidaceae
—Ligtu Hybrids
Delightful flowers, sometimes known as Peruvian lilies, in shades of pink, salmon and orange. They are not all that easy to establish, but once settled, preferably in a well-drained soil, they are a fixture. New strains, notably the so-called 'Princess Lilies' are extremely beautiful but require

further trial as garden plants.

4 ft (1.2 m), 8 per sq. yd/m, early summer.

ALTHAEA Malvaceae
—rosea
Hollyhocks are old favourites but they are becoming increasingly difficult to find in strains that will last longer than one year (they were originally annuals). Doubles tend to do well and then fail to emerge again, but singles, particularly those with yellow in them, do much better.

6 ft (2 m), 3 per sq. yd/m, late summer.

ANAPHALIS Compositae
—triplinervis
One of the more outstanding silver-grey plants. It is conspicuous in late summer when it is covered in heads of small, white flowers. It is easy in every respect but its hatred of dry conditions, an unusual quality in a grey-leafed plant.

2 ft (60 cm), 4 per sq. yd/m, late summer/early autumn.

ANCHUSA Boraginaceae
—azurea
A reasonably tall species, also known as *A. italica*, providing that rare colour in the garden, a true blue. The flowers are like large forget-me-nots above rather coarse leaves that have a tendency to suffer from mildew. 'Loddon Royalist' and 'Morning Glory' are among the better varieties.

3 ft (90 cm), 6 per sq. yd/m, early summer.

AQUILEGIA Ranunculaceae
There are two notable strains of columbines that are first-class perennials. They also seed themselves generously without becoming nuisances. Hensol Harebell is a name that strictly belongs to a strain of blues, but is now more than that. The McKana strain of very long-spurred aquilegias are graceful additions to almost any garden site and will tolerate a fair amount of shade.

Up to 3 ft (90 cm), several to the sq. yd/m, all summer.

ARTEMISIA Compositae
There are several species that can be classed with perennials, but by no means all are hardy. They are grown for their soft, filigreed foliage that varies in the silveriness of its grey, sometimes inclining towards a blue cast that is very attractive. It is best to select one that you know will suit your local climate. The most spectacular is *A. ludoviciana* var *latiloba*, whose foliage is almost white.

Varying heights and spreads.

ASTER Compositae
—frikartii
The Michaelmas daisies cause more disappointment than almost any other group of perennials. They suffer so badly from mildew that they can be a complete blot on many an otherwise fine garden landscape. There are also far too many varieties. *A. frikartii* has no such problem, a long flowering season, and an airy elegance that is entirely missing from the dumpy Michaelmas daisies. Varieties of it named after Swiss mountains are the ones to look out for, but never turn down an aster with the hybrid name alone. The flowers should be light blue with a lavender tone.

3 ft (90 cm), 3 per sq. yd/m, late summer/early autumn.

ASTRANTIA Umbelliferae
—maxima
I am not very excited by forms of *A. major*. The foliage is quite good, but the rather small, dull, papery bracts become boring, especially when the plant begins to get ideas above its station and spreads. *A. maxima*, on the other hand is a delight, with much bolder foliage and larger flowers of a true, rosy pink. It tolerates shade but is really a plant for sun.

2 ft (60 cm), 5 per sq. yd/m, summer.

BERGENIA Saxifragaceae
—cordifolia
This is the most widely grown among the several *Bergenia* species, largely because of its big, puckered, evergreen leaves that stay green in winter. The variety 'Purpurea' takes on a liver-purple tone in that season and its rather nasty, magenta flowers lack the attractiveness of the light pink of the species.

—Hybrids
Most of the bergenias offered are hybrids and are for the most part good plants. Those with 'Ballawley' in the name are excellent, but if you want all-year round green with no browning, then *B.* × *schmidtii* is one to look out for.

Bergenias will grow in sun or shade and

Above: Astrantia maxima (TB)

Left: Aquilegia hybrids *(JH)*

Right: Bergenia x schmidtii (JH)

in any soil. The best winter leaf colours (unless you prefer a constant green) are on plants in full sun and rather poor soils

1-2 ft (30-60 cm), 3 per sq. yd/m, spring.

CAMPANULA *Campanulaceae*
Although most campanulas will thrive in sun or in shade, they are so much thought of as plants for sunny places that they are dealt with here. However, when shady spots are being planted, the taller species are well worth trying.

—alliariifolia
To start off a genus known for blue, it is odd, but alphabetically logical to take a species that is white. Many forms are slightly muddy cream shades, but 'Ivory Bells' is a clean colour. Neat and clump-forming.

18 ins (46 cm), 5 per sq. yd/m, summer.

—glomerata 'Superba'
Do not on any account grow *C. glomerata* itself. It is intensely invasive. The variety 'Superba' is only mildly so but it is worth it, as it is a magnificent plant with deep violet flowers. 'Joan Elliott' is a neater, shorter, and earlier form.

2-3 ft (60-90 cm), 3 per sq. yd/m, summer.

—lactiflora
A most valuable, tall perennial that will need staking. Lavender-blue flowers on leafy stems. 'Loddon Anna' is pink, while 'Pouffe' is a cushiony plant for the front of the border. There is also 'White Pouffe'.

5 ft (1.5 m), 5 per sq. yd/m, summer.

—persicifolia
The peach-leaved bellflower is an excellent plant, provided that truly perennial forms are obtained. The species itself is usually good, as is the strain Peach Bells. Cup-shaped flowers have a long season. Seed will throw shades of blue and the occasional white.

3 ft (90 cm), 5 per sq. yd/m, summer. There are many other species and varieties and few that are offered are less than garden-worthy.

CENTAUREA *Compositae*
—ruthenica
An excellent knapweed with shiny, dark green, ferny leaves and fluffy, slightly thistle-like heads of light, lemony yellow.

Prefers a limy soil, but this is not as necessary as good drainage.

3 ft (90 cm), 5 per sq. yd/m, summer.

CENTRANTHUS *Valerianaceae*
—ruber
This is the red valerian that can be seen naturalised on walls all over the West Country of England. The best garden form is 'Atrococcineus', whose deep red colouring goes well with the centaurea mentioned above. There is, too, a white form.

3 ft (90 cm), 5 per sq. yd/m, summer.

CHRYSANTHEMUM
—frutescens
This tender plant can only be grown all year round in the mildest counties, but its summer-long succession of large, yellow daisies makes it worth keeping going from over-wintered cuttings. There are many varieties, all yellow-centred, but they may be pink or white as well as fully yellow. Doubles are not, to my mind, attractive.

3 ft (90 cm), 4 per sq. yd/m, all summer.

—maximum
The Shasta daisy is one of the most popular of white-flowered perennials. There are two varieties commonly available. 'Wirral Supreme' has a partly double formation that gives it a frilly appearance, but it is a little coarse. 'Snowcap' is excellent, with short stems and flowers that are neatly shaped and of a clear, long-lasting white.

3 ft (90 cm), but half that in 'Snowcap', 5 per sq. yd/m, summer.

—nipponicum.
If you want to extend flowering in the garden, this plant and the next will take you right through November. *C. nipponicum* has single, large, white daisies that turn soft pink. Likes a warm spot.

2 ft (60 cm), 5 per sq. yd/m, autumn.

—'Mei-Kyo'
In reality a pompom chrysanthemum, but one with very small flowers, borne prolifically very late in the season. They are of a deep lavender-pink with a touch of deep, purplish red.

$2\frac{1}{2}$ ft (75 cm), 3 per sq. yd/m, autumn–early winter.

CIMICIFUGA *Ranunculaceae*
—racemosa, also **C. ramosa**
It is extremely confusing that there should

be two plants whose names are so alike. They are similar in that they both have branched, pure white bottle-brush heads of flowers, but *C. racemosa* is fully 2 ft (60 cm) shorter and flowers in summer. *C. ramosa* is autumn flowering.

5 and 7 ft (1.5 and 2.1 m), 3 per sq. yd/m.

COREOPSIS *Compositae*
—*grandiflora*
There are several varieties, all of which are notable for their bright yellow daisies. To some they are vulgar, but it is largely a matter of placing. All are good for cutting. 'Mayfield Giant' and 'Sunburst', are taller varieties, up to 3 ft (90 cm); 'Goldfink' is only about 1 ft (30 cm) and long-flowering.

5 per sq. yd/m, summer and early autumn.

—*verticillata*
This plant is extremely free-flowering and may be found in shades of yellow that are not as obvious.

2 ft (60 cm), 5 per sq. yd/m, summer, up to mid-autumn.

CROCOSMIA *Iridaceae*
The plants that are better known as montbretia are, strictly speaking, bulbous. This is rather academic, as they behave and look just like herbaceous perennials. The better-known orange ones spread readily and some gardeners in mild areas think them a little weedy.

CROCOSMIA X CURTONUS *Iridaceae*
A race of hybrids which is presenting us with some of the brightest colours of all plants. They are usually listed under *Crocosmia* and names like 'Lucifer' and 'Vulcan' denote plants that are brilliant as long as they are placed well.

3–4 ft (90–120 cm), 3 per sq. yd/m, late summer.

CYNOGLOSSUM *Boraginaceae*
—*nervosum*
A first-class plant for blue flowers. The large, forget-me-not-like flowers are borne in great profusion but are unfortunately confined to the early part of summer. Well worth growing though.

2 ft (60 cm), 5 per sq. yd/m.

DELPHINIUM *Ranunculaceae*
Although there are several seed strains of delphiniums about, and some of them will produce a proportion of good colours and sturdy plants, there is no substitute for named varieties. Unfortunately, very few nurseries supply them, but they are obtainable by mail order. Belladonna hybrids are even harder to find but are very good plants indeed, requiring little if any staking. (See the list of recommended suppliers at the end of the book.)

The new, red-flowered hybrids, on which so many years' work has been spent, will no doubt appeal to some when they eventually become available. I find it difficult to see the point of striving for red in a genus providing such rare and delicious blues as 'Cristella' and 'Loch Leven'.

DIANTHUS *Caryophyllaceae*
Garden pinks and clove carnations have a deep hold on our affections and are among the most popular plants for the cottage garden. Their grey, evergreen foliage is a great asset but suggests accurately that cold, heavy soils are not to their liking.

Calcareous soils, even those that are very shallow and overly chalk, suit them well, but any light, well-drained garden will grow good pinks and carnations.

There are many varieties, mostly to be found in the gardens or nurseries of specialists.

DIASCIA *Scrophulariaceae*
—*rigescens*
Although this is a sub-shrub, its behaviour is that of a perennial. It bears its dense, upright spikes of pink, nemesia-like flowers for a long period in summer.

18 in (45 cm), 8 per sq. yd/m, early to late summer.

—'Ruby Field'
A hybrid between *D. cordifolia* and *D. barberae*, raised by me in the early 1970s. It makes a neat, prostrate mat of rich, rose-pink flowers, again like nemesias, but more loosely carried. Very long-flowering. Neither of these diascias is hardy in areas where winters are severe.

1 ft (30 cm), 6-8 per sq. yd/m, mid-summer to early autumn.

ECHINACEA *Compositae*
—*purpurea*
A bold plant with large, broad-rayed daisies that are richly crimson-purple. It makes a fine, strong display, especially

Left: Euphorbia characias (*TB*)

Right: Euphorbia characias, the dark centres of the flowers distinguish the species from *E. c.* subsp. *wulfenii* (*TB*)

when associated with flowers of deep purple or light pink.

'Robert Bloom' is of an especially deep, satisfying colour and shows to perfection the characteristically raised, domed, brownish-orange boss at the centre of the flower.

4 ft (1.2 m), 3 per sq. yd/m, summer.

ECHINOPS Compositae
—ritro
A globe thistle of fine stature, best grown as the selection 'Taplow Blue', which is tall and stately and is overall of a grey-blue hue that is most marked in the globular flower heads both before and after they have opened.

4–6 ft (1.2–1.9 m), in 'Taplow Blue', 4 per sq. yd/m, late summer.

ERIGERON Compositae
—speciosus
There are many varieties of this plant, all of which are suitable for the front of the border, where they make low hummocks with many short-stemmed flowers in shades of lilac, pink and purple. 'Darkest of All' (deep violet-blue), 'Charity' (light pink), 'Dimity'(dwarf pink), and 'Amity' (lilac-pink) are all good.

1–2 ft (30–60 cm), 5 per sq. yd/m, summer.

ERYNGIUM Umbelliferae
—alpinum
There is nothing quite like the sea-hollies, whose electric blue is perhaps at its best in this, the largest flowered of them all. The flower-heads are like small teazels, surrounded by prickly bracts and set on stout stems, all of the same distinctive colour.

3 ft (90 cm), 6 per sq. yd/m, summer.

—bourgatii
One of the shorter sea-hollies, with deeply-cut, grey foliage with white veins. Several stems carry blue-green, thistle-like flower-heads.

2 ft (60 cm), 6 per sq. yd/m, summer.

—oliverianum
A plant of much the same size but with much larger flowers. This was one of Gertrude Jekyll's favourites because of the contrasting qualities of its stiff foliage and steel-blue flower-heads.

2 ft (60 cm), 6 per sq. yd/m, summer.

—planum
If it has an unfortunate tendency to sprawl, this plant nevertheless introduces a steely shade of diamond-blue that is hard to match. It is excellent for cutting, having many smallish flowers on each stem.

3 ft (90 cm), or a little more, 6 per sq. yd/m, summer.

EUPHORBIA Euphorbiaceae
Although the majority of euphorbias will do well in sun or in shade, they are dealt with here, as most of them look more appropriate when grown in hot, dry places.

—characias
This evergreen plant, with its upright, curved stems clothed in handsome, grey-green foliage, is often confused with E. wulfenii, a plant that is now recognised as its subspecies. It has green flowers with conspicuous black spots at the centres, as against yellow-green with yellow centres, but the two are similar in other respects.

4 ft (1.2 m), 3 per sq. yd/m, early spring.

—griffithii
This rather invasive plant is almost always grown as the variety 'Fireglow', in which upright stems with bright green foliage are topped with bright, red-orange flowers over a very long period. Recommended by some authorities for accompanying yellow azaleas, but too likely to invade their roots. Where there is room, a superb plant.

3 ft (90 cm), 1 per sq. yd/m, main flowering in late spring, then repeating until autumn.

—myrsinites
The trailing stems of grey, evergreen foliage are not to the taste of everyone, but appeal to many gardeners. The flowers are yellow and enclosed among yellow bracts, making a ruff-like collar. Definitely for sun.

Less than 1 ft (30 cm), 6-8 per sq. yd/m, early summer.

—polychroma
Also listed as E. epithymoides. The 'flower' colour derives from bright, lemony-yellow, bracts, that cover the clumps of evergreen foliage for weeks in spring. Best in a sunny position.

18 ins (45 cm), 6-8 per sq. yd/m, spring.

FOENICULUM *Umbelliferae*
—*vulgare 'Giant Bronze'*
This is a most valuable plant, as nothing else makes such large, conspicuous clumps of tall, feathery, bronze foliage. It is wonderful with white phloxes, white delphiniums, or the deep blue of monkshoods (*Aconitum*). The flat heads of flowers are yellow.

5 ft (1.5 m) or more, 1 per sq. yd/m, summer.

GEUM *Rosaceae*
—*chiloense*
The well-known 'Mrs Bradshaw' (brilliant red) and 'Lady Stratheden' (warm yellow) fit in here; 'Borisii', which is orange, and 'Georgenberg', a lighter shade, are hybrids.

1-2 ft (30-60 cm), 4 per sq. yd/m, early summer.

GYPSOPHILA *Caryophyllaceae*
—*paniculata*
This is the famous 'gypsy fillies' that has been a favourite for flower arrangers for well over a century. Nowadays its value as a taker-up of spaces left by spring bulbs is being fully appreciated. Its great froth of flowers can occupy fully a square yard or metre from just one plant. 'Bristol Fairy' is white, 'Flamingo' is pink.

3 ft (90 cm), 1 per sq. yd/m, summer.

HELENIUM *Compositae*
—*autumnale*
Yellow-flowered plants of the daisy persuasion that share with some others a certain brashness. They are not really at home in the herbaceous border but look well among luscious green foliage and, perhaps, daisy flowers and others in the white to cream range. 'Windley', 'Butterpat' and 'Moerheim Beauty' are good varieties.

5 ft (1.5 m), 3 per sq. yd/m, late summer – early autumn.

HELIANTHUS *Compositae*
—*decapetalus*
Perennial sunflowers. Several hybrids appear under this name, including 'Miss Mellish' and the always popular 'Loddon Gold'. They have large flowers of deep yellow and are rather too coarse for many people. A gentler yellow is provided by 'Capenoch Star' if it can be found.

4 ft (1.2 m), 3 per sq. yd/m, late summer.

HELICHRYSUM *Compositae*
—*'Sulphur Light'*
A hybrid plant, making a neat, woolly, silvery mat which becomes covered with light, bright, sulphur-coloured everlasting flowers.

1 ft (30 cm), 6 per sq. yd/m, summer.

HELIOPSIS *Compositae*
—*scabra*
Probably the best known of these yellow-flowered plants is 'Summer Sun'. They share with *Helenium* and *Helianthus* a certain vulgarity but are reliable and sturdy. Some varieties are less rough-looking than others, so it pays to see them before choosing.

4 ft (1.2 m), 3 per sq. yd/m, late summer.

HEMEROCALLIS *Liliaceae*
There is a host of varieties of the day lily and choice is very much a matter of taste. The main thing is that they will grow almost anywhere and in any conditions except out and out dryness. They can be left alone for years, to be divided when flowering becomes sparse. Among good varieties are 'Giant Moon' and 'Lark Song' (yellow), 'Stafford' and 'Alain' (mahogany red), 'Pink Damask' and 'White Jade', and my favourite, which is the small, very floriferous 'Golden Chimes'. All will thrive in part shade but sun is best, especially in cooler parts of the country.

2-3 ft (60-90 cm), 6-8 per sq. yd/m, summer.

INCARVILLEA *Bignoniaceae*
—*delavayi*
There is an exotic air about incarvilleas that does not work with the shorter species in rock gardens but does with this one near the front of the border. Large, trumpet-shaped, rosy, purplish red flowers are borne above deeply cut foliage.

2 ft (60 cm), 8 per sq. yd/m, early summer.

IRIS *Iridaceae*
Iris is a huge genus and it is just not possible to generalise about it, neither is it practicable to list all the species and varieties that are available to us. By roughly dividing irises into groups that have common cultural needs and uses, we can obtain some idea of the major part that it can and does play in gardens.

Euphorbia griffithii 'Fireglow' (*JH*)

Those irises that immediately spring to mind are the bearded ones. For our purposes, the June-flowering tall bearded Iris are best and there is an enormous selection available. Colour will be a matter of personal taste, but one should beware of varieties out of which sturdiness has been bred in the search for fashionable 'flared' shapes and grotesque froths and ruffles.

All the sun that is going is the recipe for these irises, along with a very well-drained soil that is preferably limy. The comparatively modern intermediate irises need similar conditions. These are hybrids between tall bearded and dwarf irises and are more restrained, make tighter, more floriferous clumps, and do not require support. They are more like what irises were before excesses were perpetrated upon them. They flower about a month before the tall bearded irises and overlap them a little.

Pacific Coast irises are entirely different. They have leaves that are more grassy and require a soil that is lime free. Although their liking for sun is undiminished, they are not rhizomatous like the irises mentioned above but are fibrous rooted and will not tolerate drought. They certainly do not want to be baked after flowering like the bearded irises. They include *II. tenax, innominata, douglasii* and hybrids. They should, contrary to received opinion, be divided immediately after flowering when an increase is required.

A loose group of irises that prefer moisture but also like full sun includes *I. Chrysographes*, a lovely plant with flowers in deep shades of maroon that can almost attain blackness, *I. forrestii*, which is similar in character but with straw-yellow flowers, and the irises that like it really wet, like *I. kaempferi* , the orchid iris, whose flowers are as highly developed nowadays as the Koi carp over which they often stand guard.

Irises that prefer the soil to be quite wet have foliage that is adapted to their damp feet and sunny heads. If you look at a leaf against the light you will see that it has a spotted appearance. This is absent in irises that like drier soils.

Other groups, such as the regelia and oncocyclus irises and their hybrids, called regelio-cyclus, are beyond the scope of this book, but some of the most ravishing of all floral beauties are to be found among them, as well as some of the most difficult of all plants to grow.

KIRENGESHOMA Saxifragaceae
—palmata

It is not easy to grow this exciting plant and succeed in flowering it. Its requirement for moisture at the root and plenty of sun makes it a rare occurrence for it to be seen doing well in Britain away from the cooler, damper parts. Where it can be truly at home it is gorgeous and in a class of its own, with large, fresh, attractive leaves and the uniquely shaped, soft yellow flowers. It needs a lime-free soil.

3 ft (90 cm), 1 per sq. yd/m, late summer/early autumn.

KNIPHOFIA Dipsacaceae

I have to confess to disliking red hot pokers and have, therefore, little experience of them. I find them to be intrusive plants which, in their modern hybrid forms, are gaudy and vulgar. However, although I am unable to recommend such plants, there are some, such as 'Brimstone' – a late-flowering, 3 ft (90 cm), yellow hybrid – and the new dwarf hybrids, also around that height, that friends and colleagues delight in with great justification. The dwarfs range from white through various pleasant yellows to coral and soft

Helianthus 'Corona Dorica' (*JH*)

orange. They are slender, dainty plants, as opposed to the rather gross pokers that one usually sees. Their main requirement is sun and, above all, a well-drained soil.

LAVATERA Malvaceae
—thuringiaca
In the shape of the cultivar 'Barnsley' this plant, technically a sub-shrub, but herbaceous to all intents and purposes, is rapidly becoming more widely available. Its long flowering season, during which its wide, mallow-like flowers of soft pink marked with rose dominate the scene, makes it a plant that most gardeners will want to grow. It is susceptible to cold winters, so cuttings should be taken as a precaution. The name refers to Barnsley in Gloucestershire and not the Yorkshire town.
5-6 ft (1.5-1.8 m), 1 per sq. yd/m, summer.

LIATRIS Compositae
—callilepis
That this should be called *L. spicata* is of academic interest only to me as, once again, a genus which I dislike falls to me to try to find in it some positive quality. Other gardeners may find its short, upright bottle-brushes of lilac-purple (deeper and more startling still in 'Kobold') attractive. The white form certainly is before the individual flowers start to go off and spoil things a bit. I have seen *Liatris* bedded out around shrubs at Kew and enjoyed it, but cannot seem to find the right place for it myself.
Up to 2 ft (60 cm), 5 per sq. yd/m, summer.

LIMONIUM Plumbaginaceae
—latifolium
Known as sea lavender, this has large leaves of a rather leathery texture and branching stems furnished with clouds of little lavender flowers that last well on the plants or in arrangements. 'Violetta' is especially good, as its colour is retained after the flowers have been dried.
1 ft (30 cm), 4 per sq. yd/m, mid to late summer.

LINDELOFIA Boraginaceae
—longiflora
A relative of *Cynoglossum nervosum* (q. v.) but having a much longer season during which it bears its bright, gentian-blue flowers. Plenty of sun is needed and will be rewarded with a display from spring to autumn.
18 in (45 cm), 4 per sq. yd/m.

LUPINUS Leguminosae
—polyphyllus
Garden lupins are derived from this species, whose blue appears with colours from annual and shrubby ones. The Russell lupins are the best known and there are several named varieties. The blue appears in 'Blue Jacket' and 'Freedom', while it contributes to the violet of 'Saxby'. 'Canary Bird' is yellow, a colour that is mixed with pink in 'Catherine of York' and 'Brightness', while various pinks in combination with yellow or white reach a culmination in the red of 'Red Rover'.
Modern seed strains are producing strong, sturdy plants that breed true to colour and have broader, shorter flower spikes.
3-4 ft (90-120 cm), 4 per sq. yd/m, early summer.

LYCHNIS Caryophyllaceae
—chalcedonica
Of all garden flowers, this produces just about the brightest red – a flaming vermilion that sits well in the mixed border by such a shrub as *Cotinus* 'Velvet Cloak', whose deep copper foliage it complements well. It is perhaps only rivalled by *Dahlia* 'Bishop of Llandaff'.
3 ft (90 cm), 5 per sq. yd/m (with caution), summer.

—coronaria
Usually sold as the var. 'Atrosanguinea', this has flowers of such a violently magenta shade that they are very difficult to place. I once planted it inadvertently near *Crocosmia* 'Lucifer', a pure, hot red. Never again!
2-3 ft (60-90 cm). 5 per sq. yd/m (with caution), summer.

MALVA Malvaceae
—moschata
The musk mallow is a beautiful, pink-flowered plant, but it is the white form, *M. m.* var. *alba* that is the gem. It flowers over a long period.
2-3 ft (60-90 cm), 5 per sq. yd/m, summer.

MELISSA Labiatae
—officinalis
The lemon balm will grow just about any-

where and can get to be a nuisance if allowed to seed. It is grown solely for its lemon-scented foliage, especially in the variety 'Aurea', whose leaves are splashed attractively with gold. Good in the cottage garden.

2 ft (60 cm).

MERTENSIA Boraginaceae
—ciliata

I rate this as the best of a genus whose members would, on the whole, not be regarded as very exciting but for their blue flowers. Its pink-budded, tubular flowers are typical of the borage family and they combine well with the blue-tinted foliage. Sun is required, but the plants can scorch in hot conditions and benefit from a little shade in the middle of the day.

2 ft (60 cm), 6 per sq. yd/m, spring.

MONARDA Labiatae
—didyma

Bergamot, bee balm, or Oswego Tea. The plant has aromatic foliage and red flowers in compact, rather spiky heads. 'Cambridge Scarlet' and 'Adam' are the two red cultivars but they have become mixed up – most 'Cambridge Scarlet' is, in fact, the less purely coloured 'Adam'. Purple flowered varieties are a bit dull and they can all be a bit invasive if really happy.

3 ft (90 cm), 3 per sq. yd/m, summer.

MYRRHIS Umbelliferae
—odorata

Sweet Cicely. This delicate, scented cow parsley was a favourite of Jekyll's, much used by her for introducing a note of informality, as it self-seeds prettily.

2 ft (60 cm), scatter, early summer.

NEPETA Labiatae
—faasenii

This is the plant known as *N. mussinii* in gardens and is, of course, catmint. It is unrivalled for its long succession of lavender flowers and for its attraction for cats who are soon put off if a thorny twig is threaded into the plant – well, it is better than having the plant ruined.

18 in (45 cm), 3 per sq. yd/m, all summer. 'Six Hills Giant' is twice the size and is hardier.

OENOTHERA Onagraceae
—missouriensis

This is unbeatable as a yellow-flowered perennial for the front of the border. Prostrate stems carry a very long succession of large, wide open, lemon-yellow blooms, shown off by red calyces.

Less than 1 ft (30 cm), 4 per sq. yd/m, summer and autumn.

—tetragona

There are many forms of this upright, clumpy plant, all of which have the typical wide, bright yellow flowers. The one known in gardens as *O. glaber* is different in the rich, copper-maroon tint in the leaves.

2 ft (60 cm), 5 per sq. yd/m, summer.

PAEONIA Ranunculaceae

Herbaceous peonies are long-term plants that will do well if left alone, provided that they are started with every advantage in terms of well-drained soil and plenty of old manure. Only when they stop flowering abundantly should they be lifted, divided, and replanted, again with plenty of nutriment. They enjoy heat and will thrive on thin, calcareous soils if they are well fed.

—cambessedesii

A species with beautiful foliage of deep green with red stalks and leaf-reverses and large, rose- pink flowers. It is rather tender and needs a very sunny spot in the warmer parts of the country.

18 ins (45 cm), 2 per sq. yd/m, early summer.

—mlokosewitschii

The nature of its name has, as much as anything else, prevented popularity being attained by this lovely, yellow-flowered peony. It is, not surprisingly, known as 'Molly the Witch'. The flowers are large and of a light but substantial lemon-yellow.

2 ft (60 cm), 1 per sq. yd/m, spring.

—officinalis

These are the peonies that have been grown in European gardens for centuries and still are. There are doubles and singles and all do well almost anywhere in sun. 'Lize van Veen' is a double in pink and white; 'Splendens' is a single pink.

—lactiflora

Under the species name come the modern peony hybrids that are the easiest to obtain. They are often very showy and the

Hemerocallis flava (JH)

flowers can be heavy enough to need staking. They are also known as Chinese peonies. The range of colours is very great. There are some singles, but the greater part of the range consists of doubles and the very beautiful imperials, whose flowers have an outer ring of large guard petals which enclose a neat mass of narrow petaloids which may be gold, white or partly coloured like the outer petals. They flower about a month later than the other herbaceous peonies.

Mostly 30-36 ins (75-90 cm), 1-3 per sq. yd/m, early summer.

—American hybrids

A concentrated and successful breeding programme, involving species that have not been used widely before, has resulted in some wonderful peony hybrids being raised in America. They are characterised by being less heavily showy than the lactiflora hybrids and by having varied and often delicately ferny foliage. It is too early to look for these in commerce in Britain, but the development is well worth noting, especially as the cold north-east of the USA is where the work has been done, so there should be no doubt about hardiness.

PAPAVER *Papaveraceae*
—*orientale*

The oriental poppies are deservedly popular for their enormous, papery flowers in bright colours. Some of the colours are, to tell the truth, rather overpowering, especially the orange shades, and the plants are not quite as ironclad as they are usually made out to be, but apart from such criticisms, it is hard to see how one can be without them.

They have a tendency occasionally to collapse and die when in full growth. This is sometimes but not always due to the presence of red ants, who love to make their nests among the thong-like roots of the poppies.

There are a great many varieties; among the more restrained in colour and steadfast in reliability are 'Mrs Perry' (salmon pink), 'Perry's White' (greyish white), 'Black and White' (white with a black central zone, rather like a cistus), while 'Goliath' is a spectacular but pure red. 'Picotee' has white petals which terminate in bands of a vivid shade of blood-orange.

Mostly about 3 ft (90 cm), 5 per sq. yd/ m, early summer.

Oenothera glaber of gardens – a form of *O. tetragona* (*TB*)

PENSTEMON *Scrophulariaceae*

Herbaceous penstemons derive from several species and are available as named varieties or as seed strains. For some reason the varieties seem to circulate among gardeners rather than appear as regular items in nursery lists. This is odd, as they are easy from cuttings and are hardy almost everywhere, even though they may be cut annually to the ground by frosts in cold districts (elsewhere they are evergreen). Among the more commonly seen hybrids are 'Garnet', a bushy, hearty grower with deep burgundy flowers of good size, 'Apple Blossom', which is pink, and the much sought-after 'Sour Grapes', whose colour is a sort of subdued puce, but which obviously appeals to a great many people.

Most other penstemon species are too tender for general recommendation, although many are most beautiful. They are rather short-lived as well. My own favourite is the exquisite, light blue *P. ovatus*, which is growable over the southern half of Britain. If it is a little short-lived, it comes readily and true from seed.

PHLOX *Polemoniaceae*
—*maculata*

There are not many varieties of this species available to gardeners, as they are more subdued in colouring than the better-known *P. paniculata* forms. 'Alpha' is a fine, clear light pink, while 'Omega' is white, tinged with lilac.

3 ft (90 cm), 5 per sq. yd/m, summer.

—*paniculata*

Most border phloxes are forms of this species, which is found in some catalogues as *P. decussata*. They are subject to bad attacks of mildew in certain years and the spray comes into use more often than one might like. Some varieties are much more robust and resistant than others and, amid challenges from many among the long list of names, I have chosen the most trouble-free that I know. 'July Glow' has flowers of a strong neyron rose and is a little earlier than most; 'Prospero' echoes *P. maculata* 'Omega' but its flowers are larger and are lilac tinged with white, while the best of all by a long way is the variety known in some lists as 'Mount Fuji' and in others as 'Fujiyama'. Its late flowering, right through September, and its outstanding floriferousness and robust nature com-

bine with the purity of its white flowers to make an unbeatable perennial.

Phloxes provide us with one or two with variegated leaves, of which 'Norah Leigh' is the best known. The best of them is, however, 'Harlequin', a plant that is not all that often seen yet but soon should be. Place these two with regard to flower colour though, as their purplish tones can clash badly with pinks and reds.

PHORMIUM *Liliaceae*

The New Zealand flaxes are evergreen perennials and not shrubs, as so many catalogues would have it. They vary greatly in height and hardiness but all have more or less sword-shaped leaves and it is for these that the plants are grown.

—*tenax*

The largest; a noble plant with upright leaves 6 ft (1.8 m) long and flower stems 3 ft (90 cm) longer than that in summer. The flowers are tubular and of a dull maroon. The species has green leaves and the variegated and purple-leaved forms are very beautiful.

—*cookianum*

This is a smaller species and is, with the foregoing, hardy. Its leaves are green and the flowers are orange with pale green. In some forms and in hybrids with *P. tenax* the flowers are bright yellow and very striking. I have not seen these in gardens in general, but they may be seen in the garden at Mount Usher, near Dublin.

There are many new hybrids of stunning beauty, while others are crashingly vulgar. The trouble with nearly all of them is that they are expensive and their hardiness is doubtful, to say the least. One, 'Yellow Wave' has proved itself over severe winter weather and it seems so far that the plants with yellow or cream variegation are hardier than those with red, e.g. 'Maori Sunrise'. Plants whose leaves are red and yellow will make up their own minds, I suppose.

PHYSALIS *Solanaceae*
—*franchetii*

A plant that is grown primarily for the large, orange pods, like Chinese lanterns, that it produces late in the year. It is very decorative and lasts well if cut.

2 ft (60 cm), 4-5 per sq. yd/m, autumn (pods).

PHYSOSTEGIA Labiatae
—*virginiana*

A gently running species. The flowers are not all that spectacular, but the plant is grown for its quite late flowering. You can have fun by moving the individual flowers on their stalks, as they fulfil the name 'obedient plant' by staying where you put them. Good varieties are 'Rose Bouquet' and 'Vivid' in shades of pink, and there are whites.

3 ft (90 cm) but 'Vivid' is only a little over 1 ft (30 cm), 3 per sq. yd/m, late summer.

PLATYCODON Campanulaceae
—*grandiflorum*

The balloon flower is so-called because of the rounded, swollen buds which open to cup-shaped flowers. It is a true sun lover and a first class shorter perennial. 'Mariesii' is the shortest and is a fine blue, 'Mother of Pearl' is pink.

2-3 ft (60-90 cm), 6 per sq. yd/m, late summer.

POTENTILLA Roseaceae

The herbaceous potentillas are mostly hybrids and are fine garden plants. Why so few should be around nowadays is a mystery and it is hard to find varieties other than the brilliant 'Gibson's Scarlet', 'Flamenco', 'Fireflame', and 'Blazeaway', all of which are red or orange red. Apart from them, *P. nepaulensis* 'Roxana', a lovely bicolor in orange and rose, and *P. recta* (*P. warrenii* of catalogues), bright yellow and long-flowering, seem to be all there is.. Seedlings of *P. nepaulensis* tend to be well worth raising.

ROSCOEA Zingiberaceae
—*cautleoides*

This exotic-looking relative of ginger is a hardy plant and its rarity is being overcome by its being grown from seed, which germinates quite freely. The leaves are knife-like and lush and from them arise orchid-like flowers of clear, solid yellow. It thrives in sun if its soil is constantly moist.

1 ft (30 cm), 12 per sq. yd/m, summer.

RUDBECKIA Compositae

These plants, for the most part tall, like moist places in full sun. They are thought by many to be coarse, but many more admire their large, yellow flowers which, in the best forms, have black eyes. The plant

called 'Goldsturm' is to my mind far and away the best of the black-eyed Susans.

'Goldsturm' is 3 ft (90 cm), 4 per sq. yd/ m, summer.

SALVIA Labiatae

The very large genus of the sages is really outside the scope of this book, as those that are not annuals or shrubs are tender and cannot be contemplated in most gardens without being renewed from cuttings every year – a procedure which, to my mind, defines them for garden purposes as annuals.

However, they are currently the subject of a recurring fashion among gardeners of certain kinds. The best advice one can offer is to suggest that perennial salvias are heartbreaking plants to grow, as they are often exquisitely beautiful but are not for those not blessed with the mildest of climates.

SCABIOSA Dipsacaceae
—*caucasica*

The plant usually seen under this name is the variety 'Clive Greaves', whose flowers are typically those of a scabious and mid-blue. It is grown largely for its long flowering and for the vase.

2 ft (60 cm), 6 per sq. yd/m, all summer.

—*rumelica*

This is now included in another genus and is *Knautia macedonica*. Never mind, these things happen. The plant is still the same prolific, long-flowering, unusually deep maroon one it always was.

2 ft (60 cm) or more. 4 per sq. yd/m, all summer.

SEDUM Crassulaceae

Of this whole genus, and it is a big one, I would select just one plant, *S*. 'Autumn Joy'. It has all the foliage beauty of its parent, *S. spectabile*, without its harsh, puce-magenta flower colour. The leaves are fleshy and grey-green and bloomy, while the flat heads of flowers start rich pink and gradually, as autumn approaches and deepens, become deep red. It should be divided regularly in spring, as it flops open when it becomes big and the massed effect of its heads is spoilt.

2 ft (60 cm), 3 per sq. yd/m, autumn.

SIDALCEA Malvaceae
—malviflora

Spikes of flowers like small-scale holly-hocks and good, ground-covering foliage are supposed to be the chief characteristics of this and its varieties. In some gardens, however, they tend to do very badly, often flowering well but being less successful with their foliage and then dying out after the first year. 'Mrs Alderson' is rose-pink and the one with the best chance, while 'Rose Queen', which is taller, is a tried variety.

3-4 ft (90-120 cm), 5 per sq. yd/m, summer.

SISYRINCHIUM Iridaceae
—striatum

This is an evergreen plant that needs constant feeding if it is not to flower itself to death. From a bold clump of iris-like foliage there arises stems bearing several light, creamy-yellow flowers, beautifully and subtly veined with purple. It seeds itself about in a wholly civilised manner when it is happy.

2 ft (60 cm), 5 per sq. yd/m, summer.

SOLIDAGO Compositae

Another of the rather coarse, yellow-flowered composite genera that are always in danger of having all the charm of giant ragwort. However, the dwarf ones are truly attractive and provide good value in the latter part of summer. 'Cloth of Gold' is an excellent garden plant in this respect, while 'Lemore' (probably really a cross between a solidago and an aster) has flowers of a pleasing primrose shade but is taller. The flowers in both are very small but are borne in the mass.

From just over 1 ft (30 cm) to almost 3 ft (90 cm) 5 per sq. yd/m, late summer

STACHYS Labiatae
—lanata

The well-known lamb's ears is an ideal carpeting plant with densely silvery-woolly leaves. The best form for this purpose is 'Silver Carpet', as it does not flower. Flowering is a distraction and it spoils the ground-covering effect. The species is properly S. olympica, but will be unlikely to be found so named in catalogues.

Less than 1 ft (30 cm) in 'Silver Carpet', 5 per sq. yd/m,

THALICTRUM Ranunculaceae
—aquilegiifolium

The thalictrums are light, frothy confections whose foliage and habit remind one of a maidenhair fern that has ideas above its station. The basal and stem leaves are like those of an exquisitely dainty columbine and the flowers are in flattish heads of fluffy purple-mauve. This is a perennial that is best grown from seed, as a packet will yield many forms from which you can select for colour and height.

3 ft (90 cm) 3 per sq. yd/m, early summer.

—delavayi

Known in catalogues as T. dipterocarpum, this is an entirely different sort of plant, even more beautiful and possessed of great elegance. Instead of the flowers being carried in fluffy heads, they are borne more in the manner of Gypsophila 'Bristol Fairy' and are of a light lilac shade with yellow centres.

The form 'Hewitt's Double' lacks the yellow, but has a pompom charm all of its own.

5-6 ft (1.5-1.8 m) but 3 ft (90 cm) in 'Hewitt's Double', 1-3 per sq. yd/m, summer.

TRADESCANTIA Commelinaceae
—virginiana

An eye for the curious will be attracted to these plants, mainly for the unusual range of shades in which the three bracts around each flower head are arranged. An eye for a plant, on the other hand, will find them rather tatty and their colours, except for the truest blues, a little strident.

'Isis' is a good deep blue, while 'J. C. Weguelin' is pale, sky blue. 'Zwanenburg Blue', a popular plant, is all right, but has a touch of red in the blue that spoils it a bit.

2 ft (60 cm), 5 per sq. yd/m, late summer.

TRICYRTIS Liliaceae
—stolonifera

The toad lilies are early autumn flowering plants that have a quiet beauty that is all their own. The stems, growing in clumps and clothed with neat leaves are themselves pleasing, but it is the masses of small, intensely spotted flowers, like small lilies, that make one stop and look twice. The buds are brown and the flowers have

Paeonia 'Kelway's Supreme' (JH)

an overall brownish-cream appearance, making the yellow centres all the more striking.

2-3 ft (60-90 cm), 3 per sq. yd/m, late summer and early autumn.

VERBASCUM Scrophulariaceae

The mulleins are not to my taste, with the exception of the pink-flowered 'Pink Domino'. Many gardeners, however, enjoy the yellow and orange-yellow kinds, like 'Cotswold Queen' and 'Gainsborough'. The tall, flower-wreathed stems are certainly there to be noticed, but so often the combinations of colours with coarse, grey-felted leaves and general air of stiffness are lacking in finesse.

5 ft (1.5 m), 5 per sq. yd/m, summer.

VERONICA Scrophulariaceae
—teucrium

A species containing one or two first-class, blue-flowered plants for the front of the border. 'Crater Lake Blue', 'Shirley Blue', and 'Royal Blue' are the ones most usually offered, of which the second probably gives the best value.

1 ft (30 cm), 5 per sq. yd/m, summer.

Part Two

Perennials in Shade

Chapter Four
The Shady Environment

In the wild the sunny places induce certain typical characteristics in plants. They comprise, in the main, reasonably constant environments so that in large areas of sun-blessed land, plants can afford to let their seeds carry them on from year to year while they themselves die at the end of each warm or rainy season. There are, in other words, a lot of annuals.

Those perennials that live alongside them need assurance that they will get at least a few years of the sort of conditions they need. They are adapted to the winters (or to the dry seasons in hot climates) by being herbaceous, and their leaves are usually not very large and may be protected by hairs, powdery or waxy blooms, or by thick skins, all of which tend to make them attractive as well as keep them safe from the desiccating effects of sun and wind.

A typically hot, sunny place will be to a greater or lesser extent something like the maquis of southern France, where annuals and perennials compete for the available plant food and avoid shading one another by remaining short in stature. It will be characterised by showy flowers on modest plants, and a preponderance of light, dusty-looking, grey-greens.

The shady environment, on the other hand, presents a totally different set of circumstances. Because the plants can shade one another they can grow taller, and they have the necessary moisture to allow them to do this since evaporation is much slower than in sunny places. Their leaves can be bigger, thinner, and of much more lettucey greens because the fierce sun is not going to get at them and cause them to dry up and burn. The other important effect of the plants' being able to grow taller is that the woody ones among them can protect one another and the shorter, non-woody perennials beneath from winds, thus reducing even further the drying effects of the atmosphere.

Perennials in a shady environment (*JK*)

There is, too, a much higher proportion of perennial plants (in the full sense, which includes the woody plants) because a plant will find itself in an environment that is less hostile and less likely to change in the short term. The flowers, though, will be every bit as showy as those in the sun because the job they have to do is the same; the plants will, however, be proportionally more leafy.

Soils, too, will be less stony and more humusy and moist. The roots of the plants will not be adapted to long, thrusting journeys in search of water, but will be inclined to be more fibrous and to make clumps of a much more compact nature.

It is, then, not much use thinking that we can grow sun-lovers in shade or plants from shady environments in hot, sunny ones. Unfortunately for their happiness, a lot of gardeners think that these contradictions do not apply to them and keep on attempting the horticultural equivalent of trying to fry an egg on a block of ice. The most valuable lesson to be learned in gardening is that Nature is far more experienced than we are and will always resist our attempts to improve on her.

The formality that is often seen in gardening in sunny places is only rendered possible by the nature of the plants in the wild. Plants whose foliage is secondary in stature to their flowers can be arranged in swaths or blocks of colour – the colour being the object of the exercise and not the display of plant character in the majority of cases. On the other hand, those plants whose natural home is shade do not lend themselves to this kind of display, as their leafiness prevents the same sort of closely massed colour effects.

In shade, one comes to appreciate the qualities of plants, as opposed to flowers in isolation. To plant them in a pleasing way demands that their qualities of foliage and such intangibles as presence, elegance and poise shall be understood and exploited. It is not surprising that the great plant hunters went to shady environments for the greater part of their most notable finds; shade is the nursery for the development of the plantsman.

Gardening with perennials demands plantsmanship because, no matter how gardeners may seek to avoid it, a proper tackling of the question of what to grow in shade and how to grow it will have to be achieved one day and it is no good merely having an appreciation of flowers and a good colour sense. Gardening in sun can be highly successful for someone who can command a palette; shade is where it becomes a true art.

Soils in Shade

Generally speaking, perennials that enjoy sunny places are not too fussy as to soil. The intensive cultivation that we give our plants means that they need plenty of feeding, and this is made necessary, too, by the way in which we have encouraged plants to develop from their original forms. The many flowered, tall delphinium, for instance, is a far cry from the shorter, few flowered wildling with its widely-spaced larkspur blooms and much less abundant leaf. Nevertheless, the ability to be at home wherever the plant finds itself as far as soil goes is not lost as sophistication increases. The lounge lizard, svelte and competent at the ball, has enough of the old Adam left to be perfectly at home prone in the heather, stalking next morning to within range of his prey; and so it is in the plant world, where the genes for survival will not be denied.

Places that are shady in the wild are not often possessed of soils that are charged with lime. The accumulated vegetable detritus is greater because of the increased leaf cover and stature of the plants and also because a system builds up that is inimical to fast rotting. Peaty deposits form which, by definition, are acid and evolution leads to the emergence of populations of plants whose preference for their home soil is so strong that they cannot tolerate alkalinity even in amounts that are chemically just on the acid side of neutral. Such plants will wane and die if they encounter lime in garden soils.

Much is made of the pH scale (see page 18 for an explanation of how it works and its pitfalls) yet although the acidity and a high vegetable fraction in the soil often go together, they are not the same thing. There are a great many perennials that like shade whose requirement is for a leafy soil but whose preference as far as soil chemistry goes is not marked. It is as well to take it that all shade-lovers like a soil that is leafy or peaty in texture and then to find out, if you are on an alkaline soil, which are the plants that do not like lime.

If your soil is lime-free, this second consideration does not apply, and neither does its converse, because very few plants must have lime and just about none of them are plants for shade.

Soils that are charged with lime or lie above a limestone into which the roots of plants are liable to reach can still be home to lime-hating perennials of the shady persuasion. Shade-lovers, as we have seen, tend to have compact root systems, so that they are less likely to encounter limestone at lower levels, and those with shallow root systems can be grown perfectly well in a lime-free soil above the underlying source of lime – in a made-up, raised soil environment. In the wild such environments often occur, with plants whose genes have rejected lime for millions of years thriving in limestone areas because their roots are in peaty soughs.

Shade-loving perennials have not been as highly developed as those that like sun. The reasons for this are partly clear and have to do with the length of time such plants have been thought of as garden-worthy and the apparent difficulty of their cultivation. Certainly it is true that a great many shade perennials are species or very close to species. What this means is that, although it is advisable to give them every advantage in terms of feeding, it is not as necessary as a constant supply of clean moisture.

There is a garden in Wester Ross, Scotland, where the rainfall is about 130 in (330 cm) a year. The 'soil' is a layer of gruel perhaps an inch (2.5 cm) deep, overlying an inhospitable, completely inert, broken shale. The rate of leaching is phenomenal. It is one of the most unpromising places in which to garden that I have ever seen. Nevertheless, were you to see it, you would be dumbstruck by the riotous beauty of the place. It is a close mass of *Primula, Meconopsis, Dodecatheon,* and a host of other shady genera, including fine specimens of *Gunnera manicata,* that magnificent jungle plant from southern Brazil whose mighty, rhubarb-like leaves tower 10 ft (3 m) high on their annually-produced stalks and spread their 7 ft (2.1 m) parasols as a welcome shelter from the drumming rain. The secret is not just

the rock potash that is put down every year, it is the fact that the soil is saturated with free-moving water.

Sun-loving perennials are adapted to periods of drought and have to be. Shade lovers have never needed to and they cannot tolerate dryness. More than that, they revel in moisture, but not in stagnation and clagginess. It is a great mistake to suppose that any plant can tolerate stagnant wetness at its roots. The roots must live in an environment where there is plenty of oxygen; even water plants have this requirement. Land plants need it dissolved in the soil water and stagnation means that it is soon used up and cannot be renewed. Sticky soils, lacking air spaces through which oxygen can reach the roots, are anathema to plants and must be improved.

Drainage is, therefore, as important to lovers of damp, shady places as it is to sun-lovers and it is no good imagining that a plant that likes shade will tolerate that gooey patch on the cold side of the house. The goo must be reduced by drainage and the stickiness by the addition of truly liberal amounts of peaty, leafy, manurey substances. After all that, if the wind howls round that corner, forget it.

Shade-Loving Perennials and their Neighbours

The perennials that like sun can be grown apart from other groups of plants. Even though we have seen that it is highly desirable for many reasons to mix them with woody plants, the herbaceous border is still with us and will be for a long time yet.

The nature of sun-lovers is such that they do not need the presence of other plants, but shade-lovers do, because it is the other plants that provide much of the shade. This is reflected in the way they fit into gardens. They simply fail to look right in isolation. Even in moist soil beside a pool a drift of the tall, candelabra-type

Primula bulleyana will look out of place unless it has taller companions – reedy things and *Iris pseudacorus* or a small willow like *Salix wehrhanii*. This is not just because it needs a background for its exquisite whorls of bright yellow flowers but also because its character is such that it must have protective neighbours. These intangibles – character, and so on – have already been cited as things to be understood by the successful exploiter of shade, but the point bears repeating, as it is the central requirement once the mundane matters of soil and situation have been dealt with.

Shady places are arenas for the deployment of harmony in the garden. They are the areas in which can be learned the essential relationships between plants and the interactions that happen between them both culturally and aesthetically. Mastery of the shady garden involves not only knowing your perennials, but also the plants that can be grown with them.

Dry Shade

Gardens being what they are, there are often horrid places where tree roots gobble up the food and moisture from the soil, where hedges suck the land dry like the Oklahoma share-croppers of old, and where slab-sided buildings and wide-eaved houses deny rain to the earth.

There is not a great deal that can be done with such spots, where so often there is little but low, boring stands of *Prunus* 'Otto Luyken'. There are, however, a very few perennials that will brave such short commons; among them are *Anemone nemorosa*, whose invasive nature is perfectly suited to the habitat, *Campanula latifolia*, a plant that is happy in sun or in shade, but whose *forte* is in providing summer colour in difficult places, and *Lunaria* which, as 'honesty' decorates our Christmas tables. Together these three provide a rewarding succession of interest for rather longer than the average sunny border and there are others, so all is not lost by any means.

Chapter Five
The Essential Informality

It is virtually impossible to arrange formal plantings in shade when perennial plants are being grown. It has been noted already that the leafy nature of shade-loving perennials means that they arrange themselves informally even if they are planted in some kind of mathematically exact way.

Informality demands that the plants be placed so that their relationships to one another are exploited. This does not apply nearly so much in sun, where flower colour relationships are usually the main thing that is sought, but in shade it is the whole key to successful planting. Even a wide, carpeting drift of *Primula bulleyana* will be seen in relation to the plants that are giving it shade. It would not work if these were things like *Eucalyptus* species; the effect would be as uncomfortable as a husky dog in the Sahara desert, but rhododendrons would be fine.

The gardener who wants to create balanced, attractive effects using perennials in shade must get to know them for their out-of-flower qualities first and foremost. Tones of flower colour are very important, of course, and it is no good matching two plants whose leaves are compatible but whose flowers shriek at one another like biddies across a backyard wall.

Shady Borders

The border that is in shade is the part of many gardens that gives the most trouble. Usually one sees sad little plants, shivering and clutching themselves in their misery like coalmine children in reformist pamphlets, bravely and pathetically trying to give service in a totally hostile environment.

We know what to do about that; drainage and soil conditioning, with plenty of organic matter, will set matters right and a cold spot can be made less chilly by the erection of a fence or a hedge to keep the wind out.

What is often not appreciated is that shady borders are usually made far too narrow. Narrow borders are quite all right when sun-loving plants are grown; they can be planted with colourful perennials which do not reach heights that ruin the proportion. Shade-lovers, on the other hand, take up more room as individuals and need space in which those all-important relationships can be made.

If you overplant a sunny border it does not matter too much if the perennials are packed in too closely. For a year or two they will look perfectly all right and you can move them at the end of a season anyway. Overcrowding of shade-loving perennials, by contrast, ruins the display from the beginning because it relies to such an extent on the ornamental value of the leaves.

Underplanting is not nearly such a sin, as you quickly learn from your mistakes and you also learn to the full the habits of the plants. Overplanting means that you are unlikely to appreciate what you have got because the plants cannot display themselves properly. Once more, the point that shade gardening with perennials demands plantsmanship of a different order from that required to deal with plants in the sun is emphasised.

Shady borders should be wide and plants should be treated as individuals. In sun we grow perennials as groups and only seldom, as with large, bold plants like *Foeniculum* 'Giant Bronze', do we allow them to shine as single specimens. There is nothing in the world to stop us from growing the smaller variegated hostas in groups, for instance, but the average shady border will be well enough furnished by just one plant of *Hosta sieboldiana* var. *elegans*.

Preparation

The aim in making a home for shade-loving perennials should be to provide what gardeners call a 'woodsy' soil. This is a good word, as it describes perfectly the light, rich, rather spongy texture of the sort of soil that will, when compressed in the hand, bounce back to its original density, having given up a little free water.

If you are faced with a massively claggy, clay soil, whose criminal record includes the harbouring of such fugitives from justice as couch grass, thistles and ground elder and whose history suggests little if any clean living at all, do not lose heart. Clearing the foul weeds may break your heart, it is true, but what is left of it afterwards can draw cheer from the promise of good things to come.

Peat is the answer, but it must be emphasised that this is not suggested too lightly. Peat is a non-renewable resource and very few people seem to recognise the fact. However, its use in lightening impossible soils and in giving body to very sandy ones is entirely legitimate. Although copious amounts of leaf mould would be better, the average suburban gardener does not have access to the stuff.

The peat, in very large quantities indeed, say one whole bale to 5 sq. yd (m), is best rotavated into the soil. With the heavy clay soils this must be done at that magic moment when the soil is friable, which is to say that it is neither sticky nor baked to rockhardness. If you cannot manage a rotavator, then fork it in, using a spinning action as the fork comes out, and then repeating the spinning rather as if you were mixing a very large cake. With sandy soils, the job is infinitely easier but should be done just as thoroughly.

What you should be careful to do is to use dry peat. All the pundits will tell you that you should never add dry peat to the soil, but then I suspect that they have never tried it. When it is well and truly mixed in, you then put the hose on it until the whole bed is something like a black porridge. Let it drain and you can rest assured that a summer-long drought will have difficulty in drying the soil out; you will have changed completely what is termed the 'soil profile'.

With a soil like this – the 'woodsy' soil that we have learned to seek – compaction is all too easily effected. If you walk on it very much it will squash down until it becomes airless and useless to plants. The first thing you must do, once the settling period of a week or so has taken place (and this is most important), is to place some stepping-stones so that their upper surfaces are flush with the peat and so that you can stride from one to another without looking like a child pacing out a cricket pitch. It is a good idea to know first where your plants are going, otherwise you will be reduced to much cursing as you dig the damned stones out again.

There is no alternative to good drainage. A raised bed will tend to dry out and you will either be watering it every day in summer or you will lose the choicest of the plants that you want to grow. I have tried this where the area was impossible to drain (there was nowhere for the water to go) and, while many things grew quite well, I lost all my lovely Asiatic gentians one by heartbreaking one. Either steel yourself for strenuous earthworks or give up the idea of growing anything if the drainage is bad in a shady place. There is no substitute for double-digging, in the course of which lime-free rubble or land-drain pipes are laid, and even they will be no good unless the water is led somewhere else, as you will merely have created a sump.

Choosing and Planning

Generally speaking, you will need fewer plants for a shady border than for a sunny one. This is because of their taking up more room due to their greater leafiness and also because they tend to go in for spread rather than height. On the other hand, they are likely to cost a little more than plants for sunny places. They are not plants that the average gardener thinks about when planning a garden, so it is only rarely that they appear in garden centres. Shade-loving shrubs do, but not so much the perennials. Certainly, if you want to find the really choice ones that will make all the difference between a fairly ordinary border and one that will give you great pleasure and make other people look twice, you will not be likely to find them down the road at your neighbourhood garden centre. The discerning gardener will be much better off approaching the catalogues of the mail order specialists.

Such a plant as the gorgeous *Trillium grandiflorum*, the wake robin of North

Shade-loving plants as
companions. The yellow
Primula bulleyana enjoys
the company of a cousin
and *Hosta sieboldiana* var.
elegans (*JK*)

American woods, is a great treasure and one which absolutely must have the woodsy conditions that your preparation will have created (the distinction between 'woodsy' and 'woodland' is a real one; the former refers to the soil, the latter to the habitat). It just cannot stand up to the sunny dryness of the sales area of a garden centre and has too long a turnover time. The specialist nurseryman can keep it in the manner which it expects and, *pace* the exigencies of the postal service, it should arrive with you in perfect condition for planting.

It would, in fact, be a great mistake to rush in and plant the hellebores and hostas that you will find at good garden centres before you have consulted one or two of the catalogues. This is not to say that these plants are undesirable; it is to point out that planning, even if it is only done in your head, is impossible without an inventory of the resources that will be available to you.

It is a sensible thing to take notice of remarks made in catalogues about climate. It is a shame to spend money and love on *Nomocharis* species in the south of England when these lovely lily-relatives need the much cooler climate of Northumberland or Scotland in which to grow. The loss is for some reason the greater when shade-lovers cannot find themselves at home. Sunny plants can often be dismissed with a shrug (in as much as any plantsman can shrug off a loss) but shady ones have a quality of ethereal beauty that steals into your affections for ever. There are yobs among shade plants, but they are not all that common.

Even though shallow-rooted lime-haters can be grown in lime-free soils made on top of limy ones, some others, even though they have roots that are less questing than those of plants from dry, sunny places, are deep-rooted enough to penetrate the lower levels.

To be safe, then, take good account of the indications given in the catalogue about the lime-hating proclivities of the plants. These may be stated in words in the plants descriptions or as coded symbols. Whichever it is, they will save you a lot of trouble and expense. If your soil is acid, forget the whole thing. No shade-lover must have lime unless the pH is ferociously low and all that will grow is a range of *Sphagnum* species. In such a case you will have to apply lime to grow the deeply acid-loving Asiatic gentians, but few of us live in the moorland places where such interesting conditions exist.

An Example

Plan 3 is a shady planting, occupying an area 15 ft (4.5 m) × 6 ft (1.8 m) and designed primarily to be a border, but it could also be a bed. It has a definite front and back but the heights of the plants are such that the whole can be admired from any direction.

The planting consists of large, leafy plants in an irregular pattern which allows for the creation of two equally irregular bays towards the front, in which are plants of lower stature. The essential informality is inescapable; it is just not possible to arrange plants in neat blocks, nor to plant so that axes intersect, nor to use any of the devices that one can use in the sunny border. That this is a herbaceous border is true in the sense that it is a border occupied by herbaceous plants, but in no other sense. This is simply a shade border. It would be none the less so if it was a mixed border, and these are perhaps the best kinds, where *Pieris, Andromeda* and dwarf rhododendrons can so perfectly accompany their 'perennial' neighbours. We have, in this book on perennials, adequately aired the point about mixed borders, so that, apart from reiterating that they are as valid in shade as they are in sun, there is little more to say. For that reason Plan 3 contains no shrubs. If you want some, then you should know enough by now to design a mixed shade border as well as I can, and probably better.

The two hostas on the right form, with the rodgersia, a bold foliage statement. *Hosta sieboldiana* var. *elegans* is just about the noblest of the genus and its large, seemingly pleated, blue-grey leaves can be as much as 1 ft (30 cm) wide. It makes a strongly contrasting picture with *H. fortunei* 'Albopicta' which, though smaller, is still an imposing plant whose yellow leaves are edged with light green. At the angle between them are the burnished-bronze leaves of *Rodgersia pinnata* 'Superba', made, one might be forgiven for thinking, from thin sheets of hammered metal. This is the form that has flower heads of pure, rich pink. The hostas flower in shades of lilac – almost white in the larger one – but

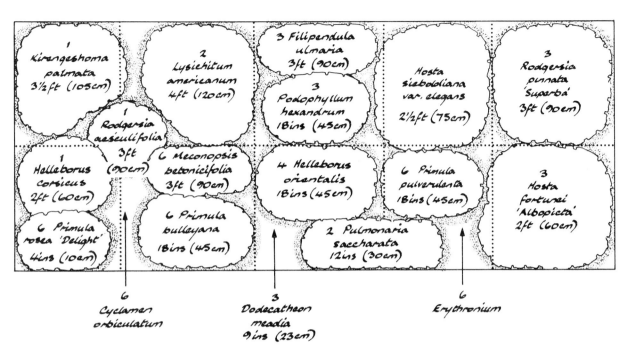

1 Kirengeshoma palmata 3½ft (105cm)

2 Lysichitum americanum 4ft (120cm)

3 Filipendula ulmaria 3ft (90cm)

Hosta sieboldiana var. elegans 2½ft (75cm)

3 Rodgersia pinnata 'Superba' 3ft (90cm)

1 Rodgersia aesculifolia 3ft (90cm)

3 Podophyllum hexandrum 18ins (45cm)

1 Helleborus corsicus 2ft (60cm)

6 Meconopsis betonicifolia 3ft (90cm)

4 Helleborus orientalis 18ins (45cm)

6 Primula pulverulenta 18ins (45cm)

3 Hosta fortunei 'Albopicta' 2ft (60cm)

6 Primula rosea 'Delight' 4ins (10cm)

6 Primula bulleyana 18ins (45cm)

2 Pulmonaria saccharata 12ins (30cm)

6 Cyclamen orbiculatum

3 Dodecatheon meadia 9ins (23cm)

6 Erythronium

there should not be a clash, as the rodgersia flowers first.

Another rodgersia, *R. aesculifolia* is part of a different sort of foliage group on the other side, in which flowers become much more important. *Lysichitum americanum* is the bog arum and it announces its presence early in the spring by throwing up big, broad, arum-like spathes in a solid shade of yellow. These are followed by enormous, paddle-shaped leaves which can be well over 3 ft (90 cm) long. This foliage is truly dramatic, as is its reputation for stinking to high heaven – hence its other name of 'skunk cabbage'. I must say that I have never found it offensive at all, even when I have brushed hard against it while weeding. It undoubtedly does smell, but only, I fancy, when well and truly bruised.

Next to it, I have created an anomaly in that *Kirengeshoma palmata* really needs sun. The problem is that it also needs moisture and it is very difficult, unless you live in the cooler northern and western parts of Britain, to cater for it. Although it appears on p. 69 among the sunny plants, I think it worth trying in shade in the warmer parts of the country, as it is only likely to get enough moisture there if it is in shade. Part shade (see p. 98) might be best. The plant is included as a plea for its wider cultivation, as its late-summer, unique, yellow flowers are very special. In this plant, it affords an echo of the spring yellow alongside

it and a fine stand of foliage.

In the middle of the back of the border is the tall meadow sweet, *Filipendula ulmaria*. Here the leaves are deeply divided and are, in the form *F. u.* var. *aurea* of a soft, subdued gold – an understated but effective touch in the planting. The flowers are not up to much and should not be allowed to seed, or if they do, then the seedlings, which will be green, must be treated as weeds (plants in the wrong place). In front of it, *Podophyllum hexandrum* has deeply lobed leaves which echo the bronze tones of *Rodgersia pinnata* 'Superba'.

The two hellebores introduce further shapes and kinds of foliage into what is a rich, balanced mixture and help to define the bays, in which the classic combination of Asiatic primulas and *Meconopsis* is to be found along with some erythroniums, which are bulbous plants and outside our purview, but perfect for the job. Some dwarf cyclamen for the late winter, and dodecatheons, whose summer flowers are so cyclamen-like, almost complete the picture. That honour goes to *Pulmonaria saccharata*, whose silver-speckled, carpeting leaves tell us that it is not only the larger plants that can be highly effective as foliage.

The whole effect of this shade border will be one of leafy coolness, but also of the interplay of interesting shapes and shades, with the occasional seasonal burst

A shady border or bed, 15 ft (4.5 m) × 6 ft (1.8 m). It is perfectly capable of being appreciated from all directions

The essential informality
of shade (*JK*)

of colour. There will be something going on from late winter to the middle of autumn, and it is hard to ask for more than that from a border in which there is not a single woody plant.

The Woodland Concept

The woodland floor, and especially its glades, are the environments we primarily think of when considering shade. Walking down from the open, rocky areas in the Alps, where tufty plants crouch away from the heat and dryness of the wind and the sun, you will, if you want to look at shade-loving plants, make for the stands of trees at the lower levels. There you will find the taller *Cypripedium calceolus* (if you are lucky) and the happiest of the cyclamen. Of course, you may on another occasion find *Cyclamen hederifolium* shaded by the ruins of an ancient Greek building, but it is to natural shade that we turn when seeking how best to accommodate the great range of shade-lovers.

The Small Woodland Garden

While those of us with really small gardens will have to content ourselves with making a shady border where the house keeps the sun out, the idea of a woodland garden can be carried out in gardens that could not possibly be called big. True, a thorough exploitation of the idea is only possible where gardening is carried out on a large scale, but it is not necessary to have the proverbial broad acres in order to make some shade lovers very happy indeed.

A corner of the garden where a birch or two grow, perhaps accompanied by a mountain ash or even by the odd fruit tree, can become a woodland paradise in miniature. One of the best such places I have seen is in a garden in Oxfordshire which is not greatly larger than thousands in the country as a whole. It could just as easily be in a considerably smaller garden and consists of plantings on either side of the path that cuts across the lawn. Each is only about 10 ft (3 m) wide and the effect is of entering another, cooler world in which

plants of a different order from those outside – shyer, more retiring plants that seem to flower for themselves rather than for show – wait to be discovered.

One of the problems about making television gardening programmes is that the average viewer has a small garden and may be put off if he is constantly shown large ones. It is, only rarely, however, that a really small garden has enough in it to enable a full half-hour programme to be made. This means the programme makers tend to persist in going to larger gardens in the hope that the viewer will realise that large gardens have all sorts of ideas that can be directly translated into smaller terms and often consist, as does Sissinghurst in Kent for instance, of a number of small gardens that are interconnected.

It is also difficult to conjure up the delights of the woodland concept and to imbue a reader with enthusiasm for them if one is constrained within the vision of the small garden. One must bring the atmosphere to life by reference to the larger scale while hoping that the reader will have been able to realise that it is not dependent on scale at all. Three plants of *Trillium grandiflorum* in a peaty pocket, receiving the shade of a tree peony are as much a realisation of the woodland concept as 100 of them would be beneath mature oaks.

The Daemon of the Woodland

Evergreen woodland tends to be rather oppressive and it is much the same no matter what the season is. Conifers make for a paucity of plants growing beneath them but can, like other evergreens, be planted to provide shade without robbing the ground or keeping out the light. They should be planted sufficiently far apart for other plants to be able to succeed beneath them. They also, largely for this reason, take up a lot of room if woodland plantings are to be made and they can only succeed in large gardens in which big glades can be made between and beneath the evergreen canopy.

Deciduous trees, on the other hand, provide the very best kind of shade for woodsy perennials. It is shade of the dappled sort – a kind of shade that allows the sun to make its presence felt without doing any harm to the delicate structures below – and its depth varies with the weather. It presents an ever-changing picture in the short term, and as the year passes the slower changes of the season impose their rhythm as well.

A great many of the plants of the woodland floor evolved in response to the changes in deciduous forest. The light wavelengths that they receive change with the leaf cover and give initiation to germination or inhibit it. Primulas, for instance, are never seen directly beneath trees in Nature because the red light that reaches them after filtering through the leaves tells the seeds not to germinate. We should bear this in mind and plant our primulas in the glades under the open sky. They will look much better there and, although most people do not know why this is so, their instinct guides them to plant in just this way.

The essential informality of shade imposes itself once again in the woodland ambience. Nothing looks worse in the whole of gardening than perennials in rows in shade, unless it is bulbs planted in a similar way. Daffodils and bluebells (of whatever nationality) look wonderful when waving in wandering drifts across a sun-dappled sward, but terrible when artificially ranked in platoons as if bent on invasion, rather than peaceful colonisation. Hellebores, spilling luxuriantly along the path of the scatter of their seeds, or seeming to, have a leafy exuberance that is fully in keeping. Planted in square blocks, they appear like denizens of the vegetable garden caught coming home late from parade.

In many kinds of gardening atmosphere is important, from the steamy concupiscence of tropical gardens to the strait-laced puritanism of the parterre. In no other field, though, is the essential abiding spirit – the daemon – as easily called up or as readily banished. Delicacy is a keynote, but so is a certain robustness. Light airiness is to be sought, but so is a certain safe solidity.

The companion plants for the perennials need to be chosen with the daemon in mind, both those that are to provide shade and background and the other, smaller ones that will grow alongside the perennials and play a structural part on the woodland floor, particularly in the winter. The perennials themselves must be of the sort that look as if they belonged; one false note is fatal.

Asiatic primulas with *Meconopsis* is a combination that has all the elements of perfection. They can be grown almost haphazardly, but the most natural-looking way is to have great drifts of primulas interspersed with smaller, compact stands of the meconopsis. If yours is one of the tiniest of woodlands, a couple of dozen candelabra primulas, 6 or 8 meconopsis and, perhaps, a backing of a hosta or two for leafy beauty will capture the daemon of the woodland just as readily as those Scottish gardens whose perfection one can only just believe. It may be a junior daemon, but at least it will be yours.

Woodland Soils

The spirit of woodland is evoked, not by mathematical discipline, but by happenstance. Gardening is, by definition, a negation of serendipity, but the advanced nature of shade gardening in the woodland style is in its ability to harness the unexpected by making it less so. Parts of the woodland floor are, in nature, more hospitable to plants than others. This may be because animals, even including humans, may pass through, making a compacted and worn path where they tread, or it can be that an intrusion of rock near the surface makes an island of inhospitality. Some seed, that is to say, may fall by the way side, while others fall upon stony ground.

The gardener who understands the woodland ethos will know how Nature makes her seed beds from soft, moist, leafy material and will provide the same sort of soil in the hope that not only will the plants be well at home but will also drop their seeds into the sort of soil that will encourage germination. There is no doubt that the most cunning hand is a novice at creating woodland plantings compared to the chance falling of seed.

As with shade borders, though, bad drainage will see off any woodland spirit, no matter how tolerant. Informal gardening is much more difficult than formal, and that careless rapture that is informality at its best is the product of hard work, much thought, and not a little skill. Of these the greatest is hard work.

There is not the slightest chance of a woodland planting, be it on a large scale or in the corner of the garden of a 'starter' home, being any good if perennial weeds are left in its soil. It might be thought that

The burnished leaves of a
rodgersia among primulas
and other shade-lovers
(*JK*)

here, at last, was a way of circumventing the labour that is immediately and obviously needed in the open, sunny parts of the garden, but it is not so. Try cutting out a bed in the dappled shade of trees from a patch of ground infested with weed roots and you will find it recolonised completely within two years. The moisture and richness of the situation make the job that much easier for the weeds and they will very soon swamp any choice morsels that they find in what they fervently believe to be their patch. The best woodland gardens are even more meticulously tended than many formal ones and at a greater cost in time – you cannot, for example, take the lawn mower to the woodland floor.

Part Shade

The misleading term 'part shade' is used universally in gardening books and in catalogues. It is very hard to see how it can be replaced with anything more meaningful that is not a long sentence, but an understanding of the underlying idea should clear the matter up.

Part shade implies a plant's receiving at least some sun during the day (if it shines at all, that is) and this can happen in one of two ways or in a combination of them. First, a nearby building, wall, or other solid eminence may cast its shade on the plant but only for part of the day. It is implicit in the meaning of the term that the plant should find itself in the shade during the hottest part of the day. Second, the plant may be shaded by overhead or nearby trees so that a dappled shade is cast throughout the day. The combination of events happens when a plant is in full sun for some hours, but is in dappled shade during the greater portion of the day, including the hottest part.

By far the most beneficial kind of part shade is the second kind. There is nothing dank or cold about dappled shade, and there is not the sudden transition from what can be the cold shade of a building to the heat of the sun, a circumstance that can put stress on a plant and cause scorching.

In maritime climates like that of Britain, those areas least affected by the neighbouring continental climate will be the wettest and the coolest, and it is in these that the combination sort of part shade is best. The plants receive the amount of light that they need but not so much that they suffer from burning or dryness. In the north and west, therefore, shade-loving perennials should be planted so that they get the sun in the latter part of the afternoon or the earlier part of the morning.

Notably there is no such expression in garden-speak as 'part sun'. This is an example of a useful nuance in the language we use in that the emphasis is placed on 'shade', rather than on 'part'. Where sun-loving perennials are discussed there is no restriction on the amount of sun that is desirable and the word 'part' is superfluous.

The distinction between shade-loving and sun-loving perennials is an important one. Whereas we started at the beginning of this book by attempting to define 'perennials' and found that the definition was a loose one, we have arrived at a subdivision among them that is much more important than any mere hair-splitting. Perennials are, after all, just plants. We have seen that they associate best in the long run with plants of other kinds to make mixed, harmonious plantings whether in sun or in shade. What we have found that should colour our attitudes to gardening in the future is the distinction between gardening in the sun and in the shade. If it has helped us to understand the essential differences between the two and to appreciate the distinct but great attractions of both, then we shall indeed have gone further along the path that leads to a better garden.

Chapter 6
Plants for Shady Places

All the plants mentioned below prefer a moisture-retentive, cool, vegetable soil with, paradoxical as it may seem, good drainage. Part shade, preferably of the dappled variety, will suit all of them, but full shade will not harm them unless otherwise stated.

ANEMONE Ranunculaceae
—hybrida
The Japanese anemones, often wrongly referred to as *Anemone japonica*, a completely different plant. They are hybrids between *A. hupehensis* var. *japonica* and *A. vitifolia*. *A. hupehensis* itself is not often seen, but plants are often so labelled. For autumn flower colour in shady corners there is little that can surpass this pink-flowered species, whose large blooms dance in the breeze on 5 ft (1.5 m) stems that are clad with bold, lobed leaves. There are several white varieties, and quite a few versions of the pink. All are excellent.

5 ft (1.5 m), 3 per sq. yd/m, late summer and early autumn.

—nemorosa
Carpets of the British native wood anemone are perfect in little glades among the smaller rhododendrons or on a larger woodland scale. The stems are very short but the rather invasive nature of the roots makes the plant unlikely to be unnoticed. There are forms in white (such as 'Wilkes' White'), blue ('Blue Bonnet', 'Blue Beauty'), and various pinks ('Rosea', 'Pentre Pink').

Plants are sent out as pieces of root that look a bit like couch grass. Plant 3 in (75 mm) deep and horizontal.

6 ins (15 cm), 10 per sq. yd/m, for quick effect, 4 for long term purposes, spring.

ANEMONOPSIS Ranunculaceae
—macrophylla
This is rather like a columbine which, finding itself in love with cool, moist, shady places, justified its passion by itself becoming modest, demure and undemonstratively spurless. The flowers make a dash at opulence in being purple without but shrink back to a self-effacing lavender within.

2 ft (60 cm), 6 per sq. yd/m, summer.

ARISAEMA Araceae
—candidissimum
A wonderful picture is created when the sun shines through the flowering spathes of this aroid. They are white, but beautifully striped in pink and green. The bold, tri-lobed leaves that follow are highly decorative.

1 ft (30 cm), 6 per sq. yd/m, summer.

ARUM Araceae
—italicum 'Pictum'
A plant of the utmost attractiveness for its leaves, which are spear-shaped and most beautifully marbled with cream and greyish white. The flowers are of little account, but the berries, appearing after the leaves have gone in the summer, are conspicuously orange.

1 ft (30 cm) or a little more, 3 plants to 1 sq. ft (0.9 sq. m), spring.

ARUNCUS Rosaceae
—sylvester
Possibly more correctly *A. dioicus*. The most impressive of the plumed plants that have at various times been spiraeas and astilbes. Very handsome foliage gives rise to fine, feathery heads of tiny, creamy white flowers, majestic in the mass. Capable of thriving in all kinds of habitats, it nevertheless looks and does best in cool, moist shade.

6 ft (1.8 m), 1 per sq. yd/m, summer.

ASPIDISTRA Liliaceae
—lurida
Just for fun, try Grandma's old aspidistra in the garden among shrubs. If you have a mildish climate, it will become groundcover. It is not called the iron plant in the southern USA for nothing. Evergreen.

18 ins (45 cm), 3 per sq. yd/m, summer (quite nasty flowers that are pollinated by slugs, but not on the sideboard!).

Astilbes in a partly-shaded habitat (*TB*)

Geranium x *magnificum* (*JH*)

Left: Helleborus orientalis, a very variable plant, is a delight in a shady setting, although it will tolerate sun (*TB*)

ASTILBE Saxifragaceae
—arendsii
Almost everyone knows these plants and their plumes of red, pink, white, or purple are to be seen wherever there is shade and moisture, although they will thrive in sunnier spots if the soil never dries. There are too many varieties to list. Buy them in flower to obtain the colours you want, as some are, frankly, puce.

2-4 ft (60-120 cm), 1-3 per sq. yd/m, according to height, summer.

BRUNNERA Boraginaceae
—macrophylla
Not all that many plants of the forget-me-not family like growing in shade with a lot of moisture, but this one does. Its clouds of blue flowers float over large, heart-shaped leaves that increase in size when flowering is over and become ornamental in their own right. This is especially so in varieties such as 'Langtrees', whose leaves are prettily spotted with silver, and the recent 'Hadspen Cream', in which they are boldly edged with cream.

18 ins (45 cm) or more, 2-3 per sq. yd/m, spring.

BUPHTHALMUM Compositae
—speciosum
Beware! A plant beloved of landscape gardeners who 'do' gardens and then leave town. An invasive, coarse plant that looks dramatic with its big yellow daisies but has the manners of an Austrian corporal.

6 ft (1.8 m), 1 per sq. yd/m (?), summer.

CLINTONIA Liliaceae
—andrewsiana
A plant of great distinction but in a quiet sort of way. Its foliage is a little like lily-of-the-valley and the small, bell-like flowers are of a rich pink. Violet berries follow. For cooler climates.

2 ft (60 cm), 4 per sq. yd/m, early summer.

CODONOPSIS Campanulaceae
—clematidea
This is a plant that is different from most perennials in that it is most at home when climbing and scrambling in a small shrub. The bell-shaped, pendent flowers are light blue, but are wonderfully and surprisingly marked with orange and dark red inside. It likes coolness, a humusy soil, and part shade.

About 2 ft (60 cm), 3 per sq. yd/m (a slightly meaningless statistic for this plant), autumn.

CONVALLARIA Liliaceae
—majalis
Lily of the valley. When it is happy it is invasive, but it is hard to complain about that. It prefers shady places but will tolerate sun. To plant some in shade and some in sun is to prolong the flowering period. 'Fortin's Giant' is twice as large as the species and is later flowering. 'Rosea' is rare, a fact that is hard to understand, as it is just as rampant as the type, but it does have a marked preference for light soils. The colour is mauve-pink.

Up to 18 ins (45 cm) according to variety, 4-6 per sq. yd/m, spring.

CORTUSA Primulaceae
—matthioli
A close relative of the primulas, and very like a woodland one, although lacking some indefinable quality. Good in cool climates in woodland conditions. Magenta-crimson flowers.

1 ft (30 cm) when happy, 10 per sq. yd/m, late spring.

DEINANTHE Saxifragaceae
—caerulea
Blue flowers are especially effective in shade-loving plants, yet here is an example that I believe has become unobtainable. It is like no other plant either in foliage (which is striking) or in flower (some are small and sterile, while others are large, fleshy and nodding). It can be propagated by division. Will someone please do so and put it into circulation again?

18 ins (45 cm), you should be so lucky! summer.

DICENTRA Papaveraceae
The bleeding hearts will all grow in sun but much prefer cool spots in part shade. They are unmistakable plants, with their flowers, like rows of lockets, dangling from curved stems above delightfully ferny foliage. D. formosa has pink flowers and is a good doer, especially as the cultivar 'Adrian Bloom'; there is also a white variety. D. spectabilis is larger in all its parts and is a favourite in cottage gardens. Its flowers are rose-red.

18 ins to 2 ft (45-60 cm), 6 per sq. yd/m, spring.

DIGITALIS Scrophulariceae
—mertonensis
Some folk are frightened of growing poisonous plants such as foxgloves, but it is difficult to see why. They are not, after all, going to leap out and bite one. This is a strain that comes true from seed and is perennial, if not long-lived. The large flowers, held all round the stems, are in curious shades of crushed strawberry.

About 3 ft (90 cm) but seen taller, 6 per sq. yd/m, summer.

DODECATHEON Primulaceae
—meadia
I confess to a great liking for this genus of aristocratic American plants. They are of small stature – many are too small for inclusion here – but they have great presence, with their cyclamen-like flowers poised well above their foliage. In this species the flowers are mauve-pink with a conspicuous yellow ring at the point. They will take a lot of moisture and enjoy part shade.

1 ft (30 cm), 12 per sq. yd/m, spring and early summer.

ENDYMION Liliaceae
While anyone whose garden sports *E. nonscriptus*, the British native bluebell, should be grateful, it is not commercially available. *E. hispanicus*, the Spanish bluebell is, though, although it must be searched for and may be found as *Scilla campanulata* or *Hyacinthoides hispanica* (sic). It is a first-class, elegant plant with, typically, medium blue flowers. Do not bother with the pink form, but the white one is nice.

2 ft (60 cm), 24 per sq. yd/m, late spring.

EOMECON Onagraceae
—chionanthum
Although this beautiful plant, sometimes called the Chinese poppy, is said to be rather invasive, I include it because I cannot grow it at all. It can be obtained, and should be grown (as I have tried to) in cool, moist shade. It has gorgeous, white, pendent flowers, but not in my gardens – ever!

18 ins (45 cm), perhaps 3 per sq. yd/m, spring.

EPIMEDIUM Berberidaceae
The epimediums are plants that will grow in sun but prefer a place in cool shade. They are grown for their foliage as much as for their flowers. While there is only one (*E. perralderianum*, which has yellow flowers) that is evergreen, the others tend to keep their leaves in a dried state through the winter. These should be cut off in late winter so that the emerging foliage and the flowers can be appreciated. All the species apart from the evergreen one exhibit most attractive autumn or winter colours.

—grandiflorum
Large flowers in deep pink. Look for the varieties 'Rose Queen' and 'White Queen'.

1 ft (30 cm), 4 per sq. yd/m, early spring.

—colchicum
This appears to be identical to *E. pinnatum*. Yellow flowers. Excellent autumn colour.

1 ft (30 cm), 4 per sq. yd/m, early spring.

—rubrum
A hybrid with flowers of bright, deep red. They are rather small, but are in scale with the small plant.

Less than 1 ft (30 cm) 6 per sq. yd/m, early spring.

FILIPENDULA Rosaceae
F. hexapetala, sometimes listed as *F. vulgaris*, is neither a moisture-lover nor a plant for shade. Other species, however, are.

—palmata
Often confused (and not only by amateurs) with *F. purpurea*, which flowers about ten days earlier. Both have heads of pink flowers and bold, attractive foliage and are happiest in moist soils in shady places. *F. purpurea* is more red in flower colour.

4 ft (1.2 m), 3 per sq. yd/m, summer.

—rubra
This is not a plant for the small garden, but for places where a wild garden has been created. It is a very large perennial with big leaves up the flowering stems and heads of pink flowers that are as much as 1 ft (30 cm) across. It is by far the largest of the meadowsweets and is invasive. Varieties appear as 'Venusta', 'Magnifica', and even 'Venusta Magnifica', but the thing is to go for the pinkest forms.

6 ft or more (2 m+), 1 per sq. yd/m, summer.

Primula pulverulenta with
azaleas in a woodland
glade at Abbotsbury (*JK*)

—ulmaria

Meadowsweet. Best grown in the variety 'Aurea' as a plant for foliage. This has lovely, yellow-green leaves that become more and more gold as the season progresses. Several nurseries offer 'Variegata', but it is not worth buying.

2-3 ft (60-90 cm), 3 per sq. yd/m, summer flowers of no account.

GALAX Diapensiaceae
—aphylla

A lime hater. It is grown as much for its 3 in (75 mm) wide, shiny, evergreen leaves which look coolly delicious in a shady place as for its small white flowers. Of great value for winter.

18 ins (45 cm), 3 per sq. yd/m, late summer.

GENTIANA Gentianaceae
—asclepiadea

This elegant plant is a far cry from the spring gentian of the alpine pastures and rock gardens. It likes shade and rich, humusy soils but can surprise by its adaptability to inhospitable environments. Each arched stem bears many blue flowers of typical gentian trumpet-shape. Best grown from seed and left to grow undisturbed.

2-3 ft (60-90 cm), 3 per sq. yd/m, late summer.

—lutea

Even though the roots of the plant render Gentian Violet, the flowers are yellow. Although it has value as a curiosity, I find this a coarse, unappealing plant, whose leaves have about as much beauty as those of maize and whose flowers are of the uninspiring colour of that cereal when ripe. Others, however, like it very much, so it is included here.

3 ft (90 cm) or more, 2 per sq. yd/m, summer.

GERANIUM Geraniaceae

The hardy geraniums – the cranesbills – afford us some of the most useful and beautiful of plants for the woodland floor or for anywhere where full or part shade needs brightening up with natural-looking colour. Many will grow in sun, provided that the soil does not become dry or poor, but it is in dappled shade that they are to be seen at their best. There are far too many for a comprehensive list to be given here, but the few I have listed will be enough to convince you of the merits of the rest.

—'Claridge Druce'

I grow this vigorous, summer-flowering plant with G. sylvaticum 'Album', which blooms in May, for succession. Its flowers are of a purplish magenta, which may sound awful but is not. They both smother weeds and are perfect under large shrubs.

2 ft (60 cm), 1 per sq. yd/m.

—endressii

Although 'Wargrave Pink' is the form most usually offered, I find that seedlings, although varying in their foliage, give an evenness of flowering, both as to quality and as to length of season. It will self-seed with a will, firing its seeds quite a distance. Without doubt, its sugar-pink flowers and pretty leaves are always in the best of order and taste.

2 ft (60 cm), 4 per sq. yd/m, all summer and autumn until the frosts.

—'Johnson's Blue'

The flowers are not truly blue, but of a solid, blue shade of lavender. It is early summer flowering but carries on for some weeks. Excellent, lightweight, divided foliage.

1 ft (30 cm), 3 per sq. yd/m.

—macrorrhizum

Like some other plants, this is sometimes dismissed as diseased in winter, when its leaves acquire red and yellow tints, even though it is evergreen. It is best to obtain either 'Bevan's Variety' or 'Ingwersen's Variety', either of which (they are crimson and pink respectively) is better than the magenta of the species.

1 ft (30 cm), 3 per sq. yd/m, early summer.

—x magnificum

The plant that Gertrude Jekyll grew as Geranium platypetalum and which is still listed under that name or as G. ibericum by far too many nurseries. The flowers are of a deep, rich, purplish blue and are borne in great profusion for weeks on end. It is a plant that is possibly marginally better in sun, but it looks perfect in light dappled shade.

2 ft (60 cm), 2 per sq. yd/m, early summer.

—platypetalum
A parent of *G.* x *magnificum*, but a lesser plant in every way. It is best to avoid plants under this name, even if they purport to be the same as the hybrid. In this way confusion will be avoided.

—renardii
Daintiness is not often on a shade plant's list of assets, but the lacy, grey-green foliage and delicate white lilac-veined flowers are capable of looking after themselves very well.
    1 ft (30 cm), 9 per sq. yd/m, early summer.

—'Russell Pritchard'
A plant of great value, because of its very long flowering season, to all those who do not, like me, have peacocks to contend with. The confounded creatures find something utterly toothsome about this slightly tender, pink-flowered geranium, which means I can only recommend it at second hand.
    1 ft (30 cm), 2-3 per 'sq. yd/m, all summer and autumn.

—sylvaticum
With this to start with and others finishing only in late autumn, a full six months of geranium flowers can be had in the shady garden. There are several colour forms in which pink, deep maroon, white, and a lavender blue with a white eye (the colour of the species itself) occur.
    2 ft (60 cm), 2 per sq. yd/m, May.

—wallichianum 'Buxton's Blue'
A rare phenomenon in that it breeds true from seed. It is also rare in the true blueness of its white-centred flowers and in the great length of its flowering season. Its rootstock looks like a bunch of small carrots which can be divided, however it will seed itself when thoroughly happy.
    1 ft (30 cm), 3 per sq. yd/m, all summer and autumn.

GLAUCIDIUM *Glaucidiaceae*
—palmatum
A woodland gem that can be found in specialist nurseries. Its large, lobed leaves are almost enough on their own, but the lilac flowers, rather like big poppies, are a delight as well. A most choice plant for woodsy places in shelter.
    2 ft (60 cm), 2 per sq. yd/m, late spring.

GUNNERA *Haloragidaceae*
—manicata
The largest herbaceous plant of all. The enormous leaves, 7-8 ft (2.1-2.4 m) wide, spread themselves like canopies on top of their 10 ft (3 m) stems. It is often called 'giant rhubarb', but is not a rhubarb at all. It likes a really moist place, even a wet one, in shade. Although from the Brazilian jungle, it is hardy, but does not appreciate wind. For large gardens only.
    10 ft (3m), 1 plant to several sq. yd/m, flowers on a strange, dumpy spike of profound ugliness, early summer.

HELLEBORUS *Ranunculaceae*
There are a great many different kinds of hellebores and it is not being too unkind to say that they are the playthings of fashion. Nevertheless, there are some superb garden plants among them if they are grown in the right sorts of places. In borders in small gardens the 'bore' factor, while not quite 'hell', is very telling and untidy, out-of-scale swatches of foliage are likely to dominate the scene. In woodland scenes, which need not be all that large, they come into their own as plants that are entirely appropriate. This is in spite of the fact that they nearly all do just as well in sun. As with *Geranium*, *Helleborus* is a genus of plants whose appearance, rather than their strong preferences, dictates their situation.

—corsicus
One of a group of hellebores that are perennial, but with biennial stems. These grow leafily the first year, and then in the second produce, in this species, clusters of cup-shaped, pale eau-de-Nil flowers. After seeding, these stems die to allow new ones to grow. In effect, the plant is evergreen. The leaves are strikingly divided into three and are large and apple green.
    3 ft (90 cm) but tending to sprawl, 1 per sq. yd/m, early spring.

—foetidus
Similar in its method of growth to the above species, but its leaves are deeply cut and the green flowers are less openly cup-shaped and have maroon edges.
    2 ft (60 cm) less sprawling, 3 per sq. yd/m, early spring.

—niger
The Christmas rose is beloved of flower arrangers, who are best advised to obtain

Anemone x *hybrida* (*A.
hupehensis* of gardens)
(*TB*)

the varieties 'Potter's Wheel' or 'Trotter's Form', as seedlings may not be very good. The large, white flowers are easily spoiled by rain-splashed soil, so a mulch of bark or gravel is a good thing. The plant is evergreen and shade is essential to its well-being.

1 ft (30 cm), 6 per sq. yd/m, winter.

—orientalis

Lenten Rose. It would be extremely boring if I were to go into the botanical morass that surrounds the beautiful plants that are lumped together under this name. All kinds of experts, from the real ones to the self-styled (of whom there are many) have fought over this botanists' Waterloo so, as a mere gardener, I shall not follow them.

However, any named or unnamed variety of this species may be expected to be a good garden plant, with long-lived flowers in bold clusters held well above the olive-green leaves. The saucer-shaped flowers may be in any of a multitude of shades from green through cream to pinky-greeny-reds and almost blacks. Some may be wondrously furnished with spots, often in deepest maroon.

Other species epithets may be found given to forms of these plants, such as *abschasicus, atrorubens, colchicus,* and *guttatus. H.* x *nigericors* (seen listed also as 'Nigericors' and 'Nigricors') is a hybrid between *H. niger* and *H. corsicus.*

Mostly 18 ins (45 cm), 6 per sq. yd/m, early spring.

HERACLEUM Umbelliferae
—mantegazzianum

Do not grow this plant. Although it is extremely handsome, it is poisonous, and while I may have said that poisonous plants do not reach out and bite you, children know that they can make pea-shooters out of the stems. This makes them dangerously ill.

HOSTA Liliaceae

Such is the utter confusion surrounding hostas that I cannot begin to unravel it without making us both suffer from monumental headaches. Not only are there streams of names in which proper Botanical Latin and a version that is completely spurious are inextricably mixed together, there are also rivers of new varieties arriving in cultivation from America and Japan. Any one attempting to write sensi-

bly about these plants is likely to have his work become out of date while at the proof stage, so I will content myself with turning a bit of common sense on to the subject from the gardening point of view.

Hostas vary from little edging plants an inch or so high (like 'Golden Edger', and some of the new Japanese ones) to magnificent foliage plants like the grey-blue *H. sieboldiana* var. *elegans.* There are variegations of all kinds and the greens of the leaves run right through the possibilities of green. Buy your hostas as seen, or sort them out from catalogues by description, but do not purchase them by name, for what nurseryman knows what they should be?

Grow them in part shade – in sun if your soil is rich, deep and moist – and feed them well. But above all keep away the ravening slug, whose slithery jaws have no appreciation of the elegance of a leaf or its contribution to a planting idea. If you have a cat, do not try hostas, as the birds that eat the slugs will stay away. If you have a dog, do not let him be risked upon slug pellets. But if you keep ducks, let them laugh their way under your hostas, and never a slug hole shall you see.

Hostas fail in frost pockets where their newly emerged leaves, which cannot be replaced, are killed. It is said that they do not like lime, but this is not true; they like an abundance of humusy material. They have fallen victim, like other unfortunate groups of plants, to the vagaries of fashion and snobbery and I fear that it will only be when they are less popular that they will be allowed to be properly and sensibly classified. Until then we must enjoy them for what they are – beautiful plants.

LIGULARIA Compositae
—dentata

There is confusion in this genus, too, as it was until recently included in *Senecio* as *S. clivorum.* Unfortunately the transition has been imperfectly carried out in some lists, where it appears as *L. clivorum.* It is a tall, moisture-loving plant with big, bold, rounded leaves and stout, tough stems with branching heads of large, orange daisy-flowers. It is said to like sun, but I find it does extremely well in dappled shade for most of the day.

4-5 ft (1.2-1.5 m), 3 per sq. yd/m, summer.

—'Desdemona'
A neater plant but similar in flower, most notable for its leaves, whose reverses are of a delectable mahogany-maroon. It is the best of the red-backed cultivars.

3 ft (90 cm), 4 per sq. yd/m, summer.

—'Gregynog Gold'
A hybrid of *L. dentata* with *L. veitchiana*. It is taller than either parent and is a spectacular plant indeed, with great heads of orange flowers. Again, although recommended for full sun, it is perfectly happy in shade as long as it sees sun for part of the day. Like the others it likes moisture, even bog.

6 ft (1.8 m), 3 per sq. yd/m, summer.

—przewalskii
Yellow flowers, rather than orange, and deeply lobed, instead of rounded leaves are characteristic of this plant. Although tall, it has an elegance that is lacking somewhat in the others. The ligularia called 'The Rocket' belongs here. This sneeze of a name may be rendered as per-wal-skee-aye without loss of dignity.

6 ft (1.8 m), 2 per sq. yd/m, summer.

LYSICHITUM Araceae
The two species are sometimes referred to as 'skunk cabbages' because of the allegedly unpleasant smell of their large, paddle-shaped leaves. They both start their year in early spring by producing large arum-like flowers about 1ft (30cm) high. In *L. americanum* they are yellow, while *L. camtchatcense* has white flowers. The very handsome leaves then follow and make a strong feature in boggy, waterside situations in part shade.

Apart from flower colour, the other differences between the two are that the American species has a nasty, heavy odour produced by the flowers, while the other (Asian) one produces a sweet scent and is a little smaller in all its parts.

MECONOPSIS Papaveraceae
These lovely plants have a way of captivating gardeners that is shared by few others. The perennial members of the genus are made more reliably so if they are prevented from flowering, or certainly from seeding, in their first year. With the exception of the Welsh poppy, they are lime-haters and need a cool, moist habitat, but not a wet one.

—betonicifolia
This is the famous Himalayan blue poppy. There is a good white form, but the blue, especially pure in cool climates, is unbeatable, save by the following species:

—grandis
While both this and the above are of much the same height, *M. grandis* is the more imposing plant because of the size and imposing carriage of the four-petalled flowers. It is best to propagate it by division (if this is done every three years or so it keeps the plants healthy anyway), as it hybridises all too readily with *M. betonicifolia*. This cross can produce wonderful plants, but not often.

—x sheldonii
(*M. grandis* × *M. betonicifolia*) Forms of the cross are among the most gorgeous of the blue meconopsis and have been seen with flowers a handspan across. They are in the very first rank of garden plants and, given the lime-free soil, moisture, and peatiness that they all like, combined again with regular division, they are permanent fixtures. 'Branklyn' is by far the best, but is rarely available. Crewdson Hybrids and 'Slieve Donard' are very good indeed and are more readily obtainable from specialists.

All the above are 3-5 ft (90-150 cm) high in flower and it takes 6 to furnish a sq. yd/m, early summer.

—cambrica
I have placed this species out of alphabetical order because it is so different from the Asiatic blue ones. Indeed, I suspect that it will not be long before some botanist decides that its European ancestry (which includes Britain – it is the Welsh poppy) will see it in another genus. Its flowers are yellow or orange-yellow and it seeds itself happily when suited in a shady, moist place for preference but above all one which is cool. There is a double form which, to my Celtic eye, lacks all charm.

18 ins (45 cm), 12 per sq. yd/m, spring.

PELTIPHYLLUM Saxifragaceae
—peltatum
The umbrella plant used to be *Saxifraga peltata* and now some wag has published it as *Darmera peltata*, a genus of which neither I nor any of the colleagues I have consulted have ever heard. Someone is

being too clever by half. It is its leaves, over 1 ft (30 cm) across and round, that are with us the longest. Before that, round heads of starry, pink flowers on tall stems arise from the solid mat of rhizomes, which is just like that of an iris. A moisture-lover.

3 ft (90 cm), 2 per sq. yd/m, spring.

PETASITES Compositae

No matter what tales you may hear of 'noble foliage', 'sweet scents in winter' or 'cherry pie', beware this jabberwock of a plant, it is as invasive as Attila the Hun. Do not accept pieces of it even if offered with assurances by an archbishop or a High Court judge. It is, I shudder to admit, offered by nurseries!

2-3 ft (60-90 cm) 1 per sq. mile, winter.

PODOPHYLLUM Podophyllaceae
—hexandrum

Better known as *P. emodi*. Hardy, but the leaves are tender as they come up from the ground. When they spread out and show their brown hue and lobed structure, they are hardy. The flowers are pendent, cup-shaped and white with a pink tinge. This is a very beautiful woodland plant for moist soil in part (dappled) shade. It is rare, but is available in commerce.

18 ins (45 cm), 4 per sq. yd/m, spring.

POLYGONATUM Liliaceae

There is such a nomenclatural mess attached to this , the Solomon's seal, that it is best to mention it in the simplest terms.

P. × hybridum is the Solomon's seal we all know and love. It and its fellows must have shade and are perfect in small or large woodland patches. Try to obtain bold plants with well-arched stems and flowers that are more inclined to white than to green.

The above is also listed as *P. multiflorum* and it cannot be emphasised too strongly that they are one and the same plant. 'Flore Pleno' is, obviously, double, while 'Variegatum' is an awful plant.

Somewhere buried under the mass of idiotic names that one finds attached to the poor Solomon's seal is a giant form, which is twice as large in all its parts and which I have seen growing in North Wales in the most breathtakingly majestic manner. I believe it to be, correctly, *P. canaliculatum*

Right: Astilbe 'lilacina' (JH)

and an American plant, but you will find it severally as *commutatum, giganteum, biflorum* and other names for all I know.

2-3 ft (60-90 cm) but 5-6 ft (1.5-1.8 m) in the giant form, 4 per sq yd/m, but just 1 or 2 for the giant, late spring.

PRIMULA *Primulaceae*
I do not intend to deal in depth with this huge genus, as to do so would occupy a book considerably larger than this one. However, the primulas that enjoy shady or partly shaded places in the majority of gardens fall into one broad category.

—Candelabra Primulas
The chief characteristic of these is that their leaf-rosettes are prostrate, while their flower stems are tall, 2-3 ft (60-90 cm) and bear whorls of flowers at regular intervals along their lengths – hence the group name.

There are several species, some named hybrids, and gardens diplay a plethora of seedlings in which hardly a bad plant is to be found, either for colour or form,

They enjoy the peatiest, woodsiest, moist-but-well-drained soils that can be afforded them but, paradoxically, they are not lime-haters and may die out on the most acid of soils. The acid side of neutral suits them best and sweetness in the soil pleases them. They do best in cooler climates but many kinds multiply rapidly by the south coast of England.

Among the best species are *P. pulverulenta*, with flowers of a rich red (Bartley Strain are deliciously sugar-pink but must be rogued at flowering time to get rid of the red ones), *P. bulleyana*, which is yellow but hybridises readily to produce orange and pink-toned flowers, and the less elegant but utterly reliable *P. japonica* in the forms 'Miller's Crimson' and 'Postford White'. The others can be allowed to join in when you have got to know these.

Primulas really must be grown in drifts, even if the scale calls for only half a dozen or so. This applies, too, to *P. florindae*, the only member of the Sikkimensis group of primulas that I would recommend for general use, as the others, lovely as they are, disappoint except in cool areas, such as Scotland, by dying out after a while. It is known as the giant Himalayan cowslip, and this sums it up perfectly, although its flowers are openly bell-shaped and pendent. They are of a clear, creamy yellow.

This is only the merest appetiser and but a hint of the joys that primulas can bring. Once their clear, delicate beauty gets into your system, you will be lost for ever and will become, like me, helplessly devout in their service. Those who garden where the climate is mild but at the same time cool and moist are to be envied in this context.

PULMONARIA *Boraginaceae*
—saccharata
Although there are other species, this is the one that I would always plump for, as it is such a good garden plant. It is a plant for the forefront of shady positions, where its leaves, which may be heavily spotted with grey on dark green, or sometimes completely grey, · may be enjoyed. The flowers are of a brilliant blue arising, like so many in the borage family, from pink buds. 'Margery Fish' and 'Mrs Moon' belong here. The former cultivar appears in commerce as *P. vallarsae*, but I do not know why.

1 ft (30 cm), 4 per sq. yd/m, spring.

RHEUM *Polygonaceae*
—alexandrae
This is very different from the culinary rhubarb (which is not to be despised as an ornamental plant) in that its tall flower spikes appear to exist in order to show off the large, creamy white bracts which hide the flowers. It is not the easiest of plants and needs moist conditions where the climate is cool.

3 ft (90 cm), 3 per sq. yd/m, summer.

—palmatum
Given a good, rich, moist soil, there is no difficulty in growing this plant. In small gardens it can play the part that *Gunnera manicata* plays in large ones and is a fine foliage feature by the waterside. I am quite unable to separate 'Atrosanguineum', 'Atropurpureum', and 'Bowles's Crimson', which all seem to me to be the same and the best form of the species, whose leaves start as a round, bright red bud at soil level and then expand to be green with dull red reverses. The flowers are pinkish red, but it is a strong colour and not as weak as it sounds.

6 ft (1.8 m) – leaves to 3 ft (90 cm), 1 plant to 2 sq. yd/m, summer.

RODGERSIA *Saxifragaceae*
The rodgersias are among the most valu-

able of all plants for shade. They thrive near water and in moist places but do not need this if the soil is deep and well-manured. Their large, dramatic leaves look most effective when the plants are grown in groups. The flowers can be magnificent, rather like large meadowsweets, but often disappoint in quantity.

—aesculifolia
As the name suggests, the leaves are like those of an enormous horse-chestnut. They are bronze-green, as in other species, the bronze varying with the time of year. The flower heads are broad and creamy-white.
    3 ft (90 cm), 3 per sq. yd/m, summer.

—pinnata
The form 'Superba' should be obtained if possible, as its pinnately-arranged leaves are so bronzed as to appear as if made from that metal, and its flowers are of clear pink. Take care not to be sold hybrids between this and the last species unless they are what you specifically want.
    3 ft (90 cm), 3 per sq. yd/m, summer.

—podophylla
The leaves are entire, rather than compound, and are lobed as if they had been hastily torn. The effect is a good one, but it is not a plant of the first rank.
    3ft (90cm) 1-2 per sq. yd/m, summer (poor).

—tabularis
The botanists are chipping away at this species, followed by those in the gardening world who would emulate Uriah Heep (a little reluctance is seemly in these cases). There appears to be a case for calling it *Astilboides tabularis*. So what, say I, for whatever its name it is the next best thing to *Gunnera manicata* as a large, round, lightly lobed, jungly-looking leaf. Each 3 ft (90 cm) wide leaf sits flatly on its centrally-mounted stalk. Flowers are white.
    3-4 ft (90-120 cm), 1 per sq. yd/m, summer.

SAXIFRAGA Saxifragaceae
—fortunei
I shall not be surprised when the self-same botanists allocate this, a shade-lover among so many sun-baked species, to a different genus. It is unusual, too, in hav-

ing large leaves which, in 'Wada's Variety', are of a rich mahogany. This variety is the best for flowers, too, frothy confections of white on stalks of the same mahogany. It flowers when everything else has given up and likes a cool place.
    18 ins (45 cm), 10 per sq. yd/m, autumn.

SMILACINA Liliaceae
—racemosa
A most aristocratic plant with masses of fluffy-looking, white, scented flowers on stems whose shape, carriage and foliage are very much like Solomon's seal. It must have lime-free soil but is easy otherwise in shade, which may be light or heavy. Seed displays double dormancy; sow in autumn and leave in the cold. Easily divided.
    3 ft (90 cm), 4 per sq. yd/m, spring.

VERATRUM Liliaceae
—nigrum
A rare and most unusual plant that is now becoming much more readily available than it has been. The leaves are extraordinary and unfold, fan-wise, to make large clumps of olive-green. The flowers, on a tall stalk, are small, maroon, and borne in abundance. It can be grown in sun by water, but is best in shade.
    5 ft (1.5 m), 3 per sq. yd/m, summer.

ZANTEDESCHIA Araceae
—aethiopica
The arum lily is hardier than might be supposed and has been known to survive freakishly severe winters in the south of England, although it could not be expected to live where winters were always hard. 'Crowborough' is a variety, somewhat smaller in its parts, which is quite a lot hardier still. They will grow in rich soils in shade, either in moist places or where the soil does not dry out, but are safest where their collars are under water. The oddest place I have seen it thriving was on the sea side of the harbour wall at Mousehole, Cornwall.
    3 ft (90 cm), 6 per sq. yd/m, summer.

Geranium renardii (*TB*)

Appendices

Helleborus corsicus (*TB*)

Appendix A Propagation

Methods of propagation largely depend on what you are propagating the plants for. The commercial nurseryman who wants to maximise the increase on his stock plants and who also wants to produce point of sale plants as soon as possible will use methods that are irrelevant to the ordinary home gardener who is only interested in growing replacements for existing plants or, at the most, providing a small increase and a few to give away to the neighbours.

There is no point at all, in a book of this nature, in going elaborately into all the niceties of plant propagation. All that would do would be to tell you that I know something about it – an egocentric exercise if ever there was one. What you need to know, if you do not already, is how to keep your perennials going and how to deal with bits of plants that other people give you.

Equipment

The last things you need are elaborate mist units, expensive propagators complete with microprocessors, or frames with gold handles and lined with mink. Perennials are hardy, no-nonsense plants, and a couple of cold frames will do the job perfectly well. They should be mouse-proof, free of slugs, and preferably facing west. If that aspect is not possible, then one where the frame receives sunlight for at least half the day should be sought. It will be shaded during sunny weather with fine netting and allowed to receive full light in dull weather.

Apart from that and the usual pots, composts, and the bits and pieces that gardeners seem to accumulate about themselves, there is little else that is needed.

Division

The great majority of perennials can be propagated by division, but division plays another part in the lives of the plants. If they are left alone, even plants like *Hemerocallis* that like to be undisturbed for several years will start to deteriorate. This is because the nutrients in the soil become worked out and the plants start to starve. It is not quite the same thing as true ageing, which varies greatly from species to species, but there is an ageing factor involved.

Generally speaking, the centre of the plant will be seen to have become old and unproductive, while the periphery will consist of young growth and will be the area of the plant where extension takes place. If nature is allowed to take her course, the ageing process will cause the plant to extend less and less and eventually to die. Lifting the plant and using its younger growths to make new plants with takes us into a different plane of ageing; the very much slower one of clonal decline.

This means that, whether we want to increase our plants or not, we really must propagate most of them in order to keep them in anything other than the short term. It is a good thing, perhaps, that this is so easily done.

Large herbaceous plants are by no means easy to split and it becomes necessary to resort to controlled violence. The clump having been dug up, two garden forks are thrust into it (often with the foot, as in digging) so that the tines are parallel and the forks are back-to-back. The handles, because of the angle that they are set at to the tines, will now stand outwards at twice that angle. If the handles are drawn together, a leverage will be exerted upon the tines which will prize the clump apart into two. If this is not enough, moving the handles apart again beyond the original angle will effect splitting of the plant.

Once the first split has been done in this way it is sometimes necessary to use the same method for the second, but it is usually possible to set about the rest of the division without much trouble. The temptation to go for the maximum number of plants should be resisted at all costs and the old, central parts of the original should be thrown away ruthlessly and most certainly not given away.

Division can either be done in the spring – March, say – when the soil is warming up and root growth is about to get going, or in autumn – October or late September are good times – when it still has some way to go and the soil is still warm. The divisions can be planted straight away where they are to grow, unless bits from a rare treasure have very little root, in which case they should be treated like cuttings and put in a frame to over winter.

The right time for the operation will vary with climate and latitude, but you will find that it coincides with the best time for planting in your area, which is highly convenient, as it means that new divisions can be integrated into whatever plan you have conceived for your border, or whatever scheme you are engaged on.

The two-forks method is not holy writ. If you can do the job with your hands or with a downward slice with a spade, fine. Primulas divide beautifully if they are lifted and then have all the soil washed from their roots in a bucket. Their crowns, each with its thong-like roots, will come away from one another with a most satisfying ease and you will find yourself with masses of plants when you least expected it.

The exceptions to the suggestion that autumn or spring be taken as ideal are mainly among plants with woolly or grey leaves. They seem to wane and die very easily in autumn, almost as if the shock makes them subject to chills, which is what I suspect happens in a way.

Cuttings

Almost all perennials can be propagated from basal cuttings with a heel, much as chrysanthemums are, in spring. The exceptions are the monocotyledons (plants in the families Iridaceae, Liliaceae, Graminae, Amaryllidaceae, and so on). However, the taking of cuttings of herbaceous perennials is a rare procedure because it is hardly necessary. Gardeners obtain enough plants from division. Those who know how to take cuttings will spot the sort of material that will perform; those who do not, or who are not interested, can be perfectly content with other methods. There is, therefore, little to be gained by pursuing the matter further here.

Root Cuttings

Some plants, notably the true geraniums and the phloxes, can be propagated from root cuttings. These are made from the lifted and root-washed parents by cutting fleshy roots into length of 1 in (25 mm) or more and as near to the thickness of a pencil as the plant will allow, and inserting them into a sandy medium and placing them in a frame.

Long pieces are best laid flat, and then barely covered with the medium. Short ones, cut straight along the tops and at an angle below (so that you know which is which), are placed upright, with the tops just covered. The best time for this operation is in the winter or very early spring. The appearance of a shoot should not lead to a frenzied potting session; it usually comes before the formation of roots. July is a favourite month for root cuttings to be ready.

Seed

I must confess that all my perennials that are grown from seed receive the same treatment as my shrubs and trees, which is to say that they are sown on soil-less composts in pots and are looked after in frames. The larger seeds can be dealt with perfectly happily in an outdoor seed bed, where they should be sown in late spring or in early summer, when the soil will have warmed up enough. I like to use frames because on the one hand I have enough of them, and on the other because the under-soil heating that I use, combined with the fact that I can sow in February, gives the plants a head start.

I would not think it a good idea to use the outdoor method in country areas where mice abound. I suppose I make much of the mouse menace, but that is because my gardening is constantly threatened by them; a situation I find philosophically demanding, as I am fond of mice.

The gardener who is interested in growing rarities or newly-introduced plants, or who wants to plants drifts of things like primulas in woodland places, will become keen on growing plants from seed. Once this happens, I am afraid that there is no turning back and there will never be a year when that garden will be devoid of plants galore in their many stages of development.

Much more detail about growing perennials from seed will be found in my *Sowing a Better Garden* (Unwin Hyman, 1988), in which individual perennials that present difficulties of germination are cited and suggestions made as to their being overcome.

Candelabra primulas (*JK*)

Appendix B Pests and Diseases

Perennials are remarkably free from plant ailments and represent, on the whole, a trouble-free way of gardening in the British Isles. In the USA there is a host of bugs that has declared war on perennials so that, even where the climate favours their use, and that is over large areas of the country, insect life is such that those of us who garden on the relatively non-buggy side of the Big Pond may thank our lucky stars.

Having said that, pests are not confined to the Insecta. There are various members of the Mammalia (mice have already been indicted) that are pests; a word that, without its middle letter, indicates which they might be. Cats, dogs, rabbits, cavies, tortoises, and several grades and sizes of humans can transform the best-laid garden into a wilderness.

However, I think it will be found that if rabbits can be kept out and if the other creatures can be somewhat controlled, the real villains will be slugs, snails, and aphids.

Slug control is best carried out by birds – encourage the birds to your garden if you wish to see off the molluscs. But do be careful with molluscicides like metaldehyde. This is usually formulated as pellets and it is lethal to all life, including Mammalia. Many a cat or dog dies, having ingested slug pellets, hatefully incurable. Use them as necessary, but take great care and remember that they are lethal to the soil organisms as well. Much agricultural land has been damaged by the use of molluscicides on oil-seed rape crops and it behoves gardeners to look after their own little pieces of land. One day my friend Bill Symondson of Cardiff University will come up with a benign remedy for slug damage; there are hopeful signs; but meanwhile let us be careful.

Like everyone else with any sense, I do not like chemical sprays in the garden. I am, however, no crank, and I realise that if I wish to garden I must use them to some extent. Aphids and other insects do less damage to strongly growing plants than they do to weak ones, and good cultivation is the first answer to all problems of pests or disease, combined with good garden hygiene. I use systemic insecticides exclusively for perennials (although never on vegetables!) and find that spraying is thereby reduced to about once a month, if that. Furthermore, because the spray translocates through the plant, I can avoid spraying near the flowers, and thus leave the bees unharmed as they visit them. Where people go wrong with these insecticides is that they use less than they thought they would need and store the rest for use the following year. This is thoroughly bad practice, as the stuff deteriorates and only half does the job, encouraging the emergence of superbugs with a high resistance to sprays.

As far as diseases are concerned, plenty of manure and good, clean cultivation will render your perennials as near to trouble-free as you can get in gardening. I am afraid that plants such as Michaelmas daisies, which contract mildew with regularity, get pulled up, burnt, and are never grown again. Rust on hollyhocks has made me banish them, too, but I use a variety of anti-fungal sprays if I have to. Luckily my peonies are free of trouble, because I cannot throw out a good one.

I suppose in a way that that sums up gardening with perennials. You try many different plants, letting your senses of adventure and curiosity lead where they will, but you tend to come back to your favourites, to the ones you know will not let you down, but with the addition of the one or two new ones that have proved themselves. It takes years to find all this out, and if this is why gardeners are said to become more stuck in the mud as they get older, then so be it.

Further Reading

Berrisford, J.M. *Irises*, Garden Book Club, 1961

Clapham, S. *Primulas*, David & Charles, 1971

Genders, R. *The Cottage Garden Year*, Croom Helm, 1986

Green, R. *Asiatic Primulas*, Alpine Garden Society, 1976

Hay, R. and Synge, P.M. *The Dictionary of Garden Plants in Colour*, Mermaid & RHS, 1983

Hobhouse, P. *Colour in your Garden*, Guild Publishing, 1985

Jekyll, G. *Colour Schemes for the Flower Garden* (1914), Windward/Frances Lincoln, 1987

Kelly, J. *Sowing a Better Garden*, Unwin Hyman, 1988

Lord, T. (ed.), *The Plant Finder*, Headmain, 1988

Mathew, B. *Dwarf Bulbs*, Batsford & RHS, 1974

Thomas, G.S. *Perennial Garden Plants*, Dent, 1982

Rodgersia aesculifolia
(*JK*)

Recommended nurseries

I have only included nurseries of which I have personal experience, either through mail order or through having visited, during the last ten years. The details are correct at the time of publication. There are many others in differing parts of Britain of which a good proportion are excellent establishments. However, a personal visit or a small trial order would be a good idea before taking more of a plunge. The following are well established and reliable.

M = mail order

HOME COUNTIES

Lye End Nursery
Lye End Link
St Johns
Woking
Surrey   GU21 1SW

General herbaceous. (M)

EASTERN ENGLAND

Beth Chatto Gardens
Elmstead Market
Colchester
Essex   CO7 7DB

A prolific source of the more unusual perennials. (M)

Blooms of Bressingham Ltd
Diss
Norfolk   IP22 2AB

The widest range of the more usual perennials. (M)

MIDLANDS

V. H. Humphrey
8 Howbeck Road
Arnold
Nottingham   NG5 8AD

Specialising in *Iris*. (M)

Old Court Nurseries Ltd
Colwall
Nr Malvern
Worcs   WR13 6QE

General perennials, *Aster*. (M)

J. & E. Parker-Jervis
Marten's Hall Farm
Longworth
Abingdon
Oxon   OX13 5EP

Cottage garden plants, often unusual. No mail order, but a friendly and knowledgeable welcome.

NORTHERN ENGLAND

Reginald Kaye Ltd
Waithman Nurseries
Silverdale
Carnworth
Lancs   LA5 0TY

Specialising in ferns, but a perennial range that often includes surprising rarities. (M)

SOUTHERN ENGLAND

Axletree Nursery
Starvecrow Lane
Peasmarsh
Rye
Sussex   TN31 6XL

Herbaceous, specialising in *Geranium* and *Euphorbia*. (M)

Longstock Park Nursery
Stockbridge
Hants   SO20 6EH

Herbaceous and moisture-loving plants.

Spinners (Peter Chappell)
Boldre
Lymington
Hants   SO41 5QE

Plants for shade. No mail order but very wide selection of first-class plants.

SOUTH-WEST ENGLAND

Blackmore and Langdon Ltd
Pensford
Bristol   BS18 4JL

Specialising in named varieties of delphiniums. (M)

Kelways Nurseries
Langport
Somerset   TA10 9SL

A wide range of standard perennials.
Specialising in *Iris* and *Paeonia*.

The Margery Fish Nursery
East Lambrook Manor
East Lambrook
South Petherton
Somerset   TA13 5HL

Hardy geraniums, hellebores, penstemon
and other perennials. (M)

SCOTLAND

Jack Drake
Inshriach
Aviemore
Inverness   PH22 1QS

Primula and *Meconopsis*. (M) Plants for
shade.

Edrom Nurseries
Coldingham
Eyemouth
Berwickshire   TD14 5TZ

Primula and *Meconopsis*. (M)

Above: Papaver orientale 'Mrs Perry' (*TB*)

Right: Phlox 'Elizabeth Campbell' (*JH*)

Above: Meconopsis
betonicifolia 'Alba' (*TB*)

Above left: Roscoea
cautleoides (*TB*)

Right: Thalictrum delavayi
(*TB*)

WHAT IS THE WI?

If you have enjoyed this book, the chances are that you would enjoy belonging to the largest women's organisation in the country – the Women's Institutes.

We are friendly, go-ahead, like-minded women, who derive enormous satisfaction from all the movement has to offer. This list is long – you can make new friends, have fun and companionship, visit new places, develop new skills, take part in community services, fight local campaigns, become a WI market producer, and play an active role in an organisation which has a national voice.

The WI is the only women's organisation in the country which owns an adult education establishment. At Denman College, you can take a course in anything from car maintenance to paper sculpture, from bookbinding to yoga, or *cordon bleu* cookery to fly-fishing.

All you need to do to join is write to us here at the National Federation of Women's Institutes, 39 Eccleston Street, London SW1W 9NT, or telephone 01-730 7212, and we will put you in touch with WIs in your immediate locality. We hope to hear from you.

Index

Page references in italics are to captions

OTHER BOOKS IN THE WI CREATIVE GARDENING SERIES

BULBS
Christine Skelmersdale

Gorgeously illustrated and enthusiastically written, this guide takes the chance factor out of choosing the best bulbs to suit the habitat of your garden – whether a sunny border, shady corner, woodland, lawn – or to meet the special requirements of rockeries or container planting.

The author shows how the creative use of bulbs can enhance the ambience of the whole garden. She demonstrates the use of bulbs to extend the flowering season, particularly in winter, or to add specific touches of colour and texture. Here is a book that will be a help and an inspiration to all gardeners.

Lady Skelmersdale runs Broadleigh Gardens in Somerset, a nursery specialising in the smaller bulbs, woodland and foliage plants.

TO BE PUBLISHED IN THE AUTUMN:

TREES AND SHRUBS
by John Kelly

ALPINES
by Jack Elliott

Both lavishly illustrated, the next two titles in the series offer practical, down to earth advice. Designed to encourage gardeners to experiment, each book takes one element in the harmonious community of plants that is the essence of a balanced and successful garden.

WI EVERYWOMAN GUIDES

These guides are a new series of practical reference guides specially designed to meet the needs of women today. Exceptionally clear and readable, they provide authoritative expert advice and guidance on topics from health to insurance: covering the options available, your rights, and how to ensure that you are getting the best possible deal.

The guides focus on topics of vital importance to women of all ages and lifestyles, and their easy-to-use reference format means that they can be dipped into to provide on-the-spot advice for specific problems.

WOMEN AND MEDICAL CARE
Lee Rodwell

Women and Medical Care clearly outlines the medical care provisions available to women today and explains how the system works with the NHS and the private sector. It gives a guide to the people within the medical services from GP and Community Nurse to Specialist and Consultant. Included is an A-Z of women's health problems with down to earth advice on what action to take and a section on alternative and complementary medicine. Also included is a comprehensive list of useful names and addresses.

Lee Rodwell contributes to the health pages of numerous newspapers and magazines including *The Times* and the *Independent*.

WOMEN AND CONSUMER RIGHTS
Cassandra Kent

This clear practical guide outlines the rights, concessions and services that are available to women today.

Women and Consumer Rights offers explanations and down to earth advice on how you can ensure that you are getting the best deal available from local government, professionals, retailers and services. It gives advice on mail order shopping, buying secondhand, auctions, employment, insurance, financial schemes and many other topics.

Complete with useful addresses, this is an essential reference book to steer you through today's complex bureaucracy.

Cassandra Kent is Consumer Affairs Editor of *Good Housekeeping*.

WOMEN AND INSURANCE
Wendy Elkington

Women and Insurance outlines the reasons for buying insurance, explains the different advantages offered by the wide variety of insurance available and gives guidance on choosing the right policy to suit your needs. There is background information on who needs insurance, who sells insurance, types of companies, the importance of planning and consumer protection. Also included is advice on specific schemes such as those for investment, mortgages, pensions and the home. There are case studies, useful addresses and practical advice in everyday language, making this an essential reference book.

Wendy Elkington is Deputy Editor of Money Mail in the *Daily Mail*.

WOMEN AND EMPLOYMENT
Jane McLoughlin

Women and Employment offers practical advice on employment possibilities for women today, whether it is a first job or returning to work after the birth of your child or in later life when the family have grown up. There are guidelines on flexi-time, job-sharing, temping, part-time and freelance work, employing others at home and in the workplace and the role of women in management. Included are explanations of conditions and rights and help in planning a career.

This invaluable reference book also contains a list of useful addresses.

Jane McLoughlin is a journalist and former Editor of the *Guardian's* women's page.

Bulbs Christine Skelmersdale	£10.95	☐
Trees and Shrubs John Kelly	£10.95	☐
Alpines Jack Elliott	£10.95	☐
Women and Medical Care Lee Rodwell	£3.50	☐
Women and Consumer Rights Cassandra Kent	£3.50	☐
Women and Insurance Wendy Elkington	£3.50	☐
Women and Employment Jane McLoughlin	£3.50	☐

All these books are available at your local bookshop or newsagent, or can be ordered direct by post. Just tick the titles you want and fill in the form below.

Name ....

Address..

....

....

Write to Unwin Cash Sales, PO Box 11, Falmouth, Cornwall TR10 9EN. Please enclose remittance to the value of the cover price plus:

UK: 60p for the first book plus 25p for the second book, thereafter 15p for each additional book ordered to a maximum charge of £1.90.

BFPO: 60p for the first book plus 25p for the second book and 15p for the next 7 books and thereafter 9p per book.

OVERSEAS INCLUDING EIRE: £1.25 for the first book plus 75p for the second book and 28p for each additional book.

Unwin Hyman reserve the right to show new retail prices on covers, which may differ from those previously advertised in the text or elsewhere. Postage rates are also subject to revision.